"Tobby Smith's *Wolfology* is a sies and theological controve: threats to orthodoxy lay persons within the church will encounter or ask questions about with plain language and pastoral concern. Any individual Christian or small group who wants to explore a brief overview of these topics will benefit from this book!"

Rhyne Putnam
Associate Professor of Theology and Culture, New Orleans Baptist Theological Seminary

"[*Wolfology*] is a whirlwind trek through various currents of thought sourcing American culture. Tobby Smith has identified both the streams feeding cultural narratives and traced those streams back to their fountainheads—sometimes going back centuries to discover the source...All in all, readers will be better informed both about their culture and about their faith in Christ after completing this book."

Greg Cochran
Director of Applied Theology, California Baptist University

"Tobby Smith has written a very accurate and readable introduction to heresies in the church, to the wolves in sheep's clothing, that encompasses heresies both ancient and modern. In doing so, he demonstrates that ancient false teachings in the church have a way of popping up over and over again. He does all of this in a winsome style that makes you think you are having this discussion over coffee and pancakes at Waffle House...these chapters were formulated not in an ivory tower where a monk is simply poring over ancient documents. They were formulated in pastoral preaching in a local congregation. Here is pastoral theology at its best."

Chad Owen Brand
Formerly Professor of Christian Theology, The Southern Baptist Theological Seminary

"Tobby confronts many issues affecting the Church with biblical and theological clarity and precision to help people spot theological error and know and love the truth. *Wolfology* helps Christians uncover error going around us, which isn't new but old...Whether you are a new or seasoned Christian, *Wolfology* will help you understand these issues and will most importantly help you learn to spot those pretending to stand on the side of truth but who are not."

Dave Jenkins
Founder and Executive Director, Servants of Grace, Executive Editor, *Theology for Life Magazine*, Host and Producer, Equipping You in Grace, Author, *The Word Explored: The Problem of Biblical Illiteracy and What To Do About It*

WOLFOLOGY

A Look at Heresies, Old and New

Tobby E. Smith

ISBN: 978-1-934952-58-0

DEDICATION

To the bride of my youth, Rachel Gail. You have always been my
hopeful. May the Lord grant us safe passage on
our way to the Celestial city.

And to my son, Piper. Be faithful to the end, like brave Tirian who
stood firm in Narnia's final days.

Acknowledgements

This book is the outworking of a preaching series that I delivered for a period of several weeks in early 2019 at my home church—Memorial Baptist Church, New Castle, Indiana. The leadership of MBC, and the congregational support that I have received from the people I preach to each week made me think that other believers could benefit from a practical and pastoral resource on both ancient and modern heresies. So, to the beloved saints of MBC I want to say thank you. Every ounce of encouragement you gave me moved me one step closer to the finish line.

Likewise, I want to thank my wife for her immense support throughout the writing process: praying for me, encouraging me, feeding me, brainstorming with me, and sometimes even prodding me to move. Additionally, my son, Piper, has taken a keen interest in the subject matter and it has propelled me in more ways than he probably realizes right now. Furthermore, I want to thank my nephew's dear wife, Sam Vaughn, for her work on the book cover.

I cannot fail to express gratitude to the hard work and diligence of Shaun Dufault. Shaun read thoroughly through the manuscript correcting my mistakes and ironing out several kinks along the way. Lastly, I want to say thank you to Rick Kress for giving me the opportunity to publish under his banner. I hope that this project proves worthy of the time, investment, ink, and paper.

Tobby E. Smith
New Castle, Indiana
March, 2021

Contents

Contents

Beware of false prophets, who come to you in sheep's clothing but inwardly are ravenous wolves.

—Jesus of Nazareth (Mt 7:15)

Introduction

Imagine what life would be like if we were only flesh without a skeleton. We would be nothing more than a puddle of blood and skin, basically, a human ravioli. This is not a pretty way to start a book, but you get the picture. A body without bones is but a useless pile of red-jelly. Just as skin and muscle are built on a skeletal system, so the believer's faith is built on the unyielding nature of Christian teaching. Without doctrine, Christianity devolves into spiritual gobbledygook. Lean in for a moment and read carefully the following words: *sound doctrine is deadly serious* and *false doctrine is seriously deadly.*

In the West, there is a torrent of shallow and superficial Christianity. Few people would deny that. Unsurprisingly, you can view YouTube clips of celebrity pastors making statements that are far outside the frame of Christian orthodoxy and much more in line with both ancient and modern heresies. So, doctrinal discernment is essential to the life of the church.

Some believers might be reading this and thinking, *"No. I am one of those non-doctrinal Christians. I really just need Jesus, and that's enough for me."* That sounds well-meaning, but it also trivializes the emphasis that Scripture places on sound doctrine (Titus 1:9; 2:1; 2 Tim 4:2-4). An attempt at non-doctrinal Christianity is like a scuba diver who holds oxygen tanks in contempt and refuses to wear them. You could try to dive without tanks, but you won't get far, and you might die. Good theology is not an option for believers; it is essential.

In our pursuit of good theology, we find ourselves taking a few steps backwards, looking through the corridors of our past and what we soon discover is that Christian doctrines developed and were organized over time. Now, there is no dispute to the authority and inerrancy of Scripture between these pages. At the same time, Scripture did not come with an organized system of theological thought. Early church history shows the Church Fathers (the Patristic writers) wrestling with the apostolic faith and organizing the theology found in the Scriptures.

While Christian doctrine was in the process of development there was an emergence of *wolfish teachers*. These wolfish teachers had been thorns in the sides of the Apostles as well, but they multiplied like Gremlins. These wolves made formidable challenges to even the most learned of Christian theologians and philosophers. But before we get too ahead of ourselves, it might be useful to define two key terms in this book that the reader will need to be familiar with, namely: *orthodoxy* and *heresy*.

Orthodoxy is the essential truths of Christianity as revealed in the Scriptures. Any addition or deviation from orthodoxy and the nature of the Christian religion changes from orthodoxy into another category, what we call heresy.

Heresy is the business of wolves. Biologist, David Mech, explained the nature of wolves in the following way, "The wolf is a large wild dog. It hunts, it pursues, attacks, kills, and eats animals larger than itself."[1] Wolves are intelligent, they can adapt to their surroundings well, and they have massive jaws filled with razor-sharp teeth. That is why it is not surprising that Jesus draws upon the imagery of wolves to convey the horror of false teachers and those who would pervert His doctrines. This is also why Jesus warns His church to stay alert, remain awake, and to be vigilant, *which is why I wrote this book*.

Wolfology does not approach the subject matter with the intentions of mischaracterizing or sensationalizing. Instead, this book attempts to make an honest assessment of both the individuals and the movements. Additionally, I write this book with the conviction that *heresy is the great teacher of orthodoxy. Heresy begins where orthodoxy ends.*

By examining some of the attributes of movements that have attempted to subvert Christianity, either intentionally or inadvertently, believers will be able to commune more intimately with the One who is not only the Truth, but also our very Life. It is time to get serious about seriously deadly doctrine. Let's begin.

Jesus Christ is the same yesterday, today, and forever.

—Hebrews 13:8

Arianism

"There was a time when he was not." It does not sound catchy, but in the 4th century a great many shipbuilders and sailors sang that tune as vigorously as my friends sang "Ice-Ice-Baby" in the early 1990s. The funky jams of Vanilla Ice were only in bad taste, but the shanty songs of the sailors consisted of bad theology. This chapter reaches back in time to one of the earliest heresies of the church—*Arianism* (not to be confused with Nazi Aryanism). Arianism is the false teaching that denied Jesus's divinity.

Arianism got its name from a man named Arius, a priest from Antioch. At the time, Antioch was an important center for learning the art of biblical interpretation (hermeneutics). The school's method of biblical analysis was to interpret Scripture with a rigid literalism. Arius tutored under the school's master, Lucian. In time, Arius became a gifted orator who set about applying his biblical hermeneutics to his preaching ministry. Eventually, Arius left the school in Antioch to take on a priestly office near the Great Harbour in Alexandria, Egypt in A.D. 314.

Alexandria had its school of biblical interpretation too, which was more in line with the church father, Origen. Where Antioch tended towards hyper-literalism, Alexandria approached Scripture allegorically. The allegorical interpreters viewed the Bible in three senses: first, the literal sense (what it plainly says); second, the moral sense (what it means for practical application); and third, the allegorical sense (the spiritual sense). It is important to note that the Alexandrians did not deny the plain meaning of the text. It just meant that they approached the Bible the way many children of my generation approached *Cracker Jacks*. We did not care about the popcorn at the top (the plain meaning of the text). We raced to the bottom to get the prize (the "deeper meaning"). Many of the problems that eventually arose came as a result of these two competing biblical interpretations.

The nature of the church is vital to consider when examining the Arian controversy. During the 4th century, bishops served as the watchmen for the cities' doctrinal purity; sort of like spiritual sheriffs. Arius was assigned to be a priest in one of the districts of Alexandria under the careful eye of Bishop Alexander. Alexander took a liking to Arius right away. By all accounts, Arius could preach and teach well. He had a popular style for the time, which helped him gain substantial influence over his parish. Arius may have been a foreshadow of the celebrity preacher who starts with a strong foundation of Christian teaching at the core of his ministry but drifts into apostasy over time. The old principle is true: *you cannot drift into orthodoxy, but you can drift into heresy.* Such was the case with Arius.

ARIUS' HERESY

Arius began teaching that not only was Jesus less than God, but also that Jesus was not of the same substance of God (*homoiousios*). For Arius, Jesus may have been more than man, but He was certainly not equal with God. In Arius' theology, Jesus was like God, but not the same as God. Now one thing you need to understand about heretics is this: they may be wolves, but they are not the evil-comic-villains that Christians sometimes make them out to be. It is not like heretics are demonic trolls who drink the blood of baby chickens at Black Masses. Instead, the turn toward false doctrine is usually an attempt to preserve or protect another critical doctrine. It can be compared to having a slight ankle sprain and overcompensating with the other leg, which creates back and hip pain. It is what happens when to fix one problem you end up creating a larger problem.

What exactly was Arius trying to protect? Three specific tenets: one, the monotheistic nature of God; two, the impassibility of God; and three, the immutability of God.

Arius Tries to Protect Monotheism

Part of Arius' concern was that he considered Bishop Alexander's teaching upon the nature of Jesus to closely align with Sabellianism. Sabellianism (a heresy we will look at in a couple of chapters) is the view that God is one but operates in three successive modes: The Father-mode, The Son-mode, and The Spirit-mode. This would mean that the continuity between Judaism and Christianity upon the monotheistic nature of God would be in peril.

Arius Tries to Preserve God's Immutability

Arius was not only trying to protect God's monotheism, but he was also trying to preserve the doctrine of God's immutability. God's immutability is the scriptural teaching that God's nature does not change (Ps 102:26). For example, God does not change His plans; His eternal decrees do not change; God does not grow old; nor does He ever learn new information. A.W. Pink put it this way, "God cannot change for the better, for he is already perfect; and, being perfect, God cannot change for the worse."[1] Christians take a lot of comfort from the thought of the God who does not change.

However, in Arius's frame of understanding, he thought that if Jesus existed eternally as God and then became a man, it would injure God's immutability. Arius surveyed the life of Christ and observed that Jesus was born as a baby, grew physically, and grew in knowledge; Jesus had emotions too. From Arius' perspective, if God could change His form, then He could also change His mind. Arius thought that the implications would be devastating to Christianity. After all, *how can anyone trust a God who changes? How can anyone know a God who changes?*

3

Arius' solution was to teach that Christ held a special place in the plan of redemption, but that Jesus did not have the same nature of God (was not *homoiousios*). In other words, Christ was like God just not the same as God. Thus, Jesus was not co-eternal with God. It's one of the reasons Arius' song *Thalia* went to the top of the pop charts in Alexandria. Arius had a straightforward interpretation of Scripture that blue collar men could understand and even easily sing, *"There was a time when Jesus was not."*

Arius Tries to Protect God's Impassibility

Arius was also concerned with the doctrine of God's impassibility. Impassibility, according to theologian Mark Jones, means, "No external agent can affect God to the point that God changes His being."[2] So, impassibility does not mean that God is some austere, passionless, divine Terminator. Instead, it means no outside forces can affect God to the point where He changes His nature, His mind, or His divine decree. Outside forces change human beings all the time and make them act in ways they never thought they could, but external forces never change God.

However, Arius could not reconcile the concept of Jesus's deity with God's impassibility. After all, Jesus was moved to tears when He stood at Lazarus' tomb; Jesus bewailed the blindness of the religious hypocrites of Jerusalem, and while Jesus was suffocating on the cross He cried out, "My God, my God why have you forsaken me (Mt 27:46)." Arius' rationalism steered him to wrongly conclude that though Jesus held a special place within Christendom, He does not share the same essence as God the Father.

A SPLINTERED CHURCH

Arius' doctrines spread like wildfire. However, in trying to fix one theological dilemma, Arius created a whole new one. At first, Arius attempted debating Bishop Alexander diplomatically, explaining to his spiritual authority in a letter:

To our blessed pope and bishop Alexander, the presbyter and deacons send greetings in the Lord. Our faith which we received from our forefathers and have also learned from you is this. We know there is one God, the only unbegotten, only eternal, only without beginning, only true, who only has immortality...Before everlasting ages he begot his unique Son, through whom he made the ages and all things...a perfect creature of God... [the Son] is neither eternal nor co-eternal nor unbegotten of the Father.[3]

Bishop Alexander, along with his young protégé Athanasius, would meet Arius head-on in a battle that would last nearly fifty years. The bishop responded to Arius' accusations with accusations of his own. Alexander charged Arius with "degrading the Son to the rank of a creature."[4]

Ironically, Alexander had emphasized the immutability of God in his arguments, explaining that to adopt Arius' views not only meant that the Son was not co-eternal with God, but that there was also a time that God was not always Father. Alexander's argument went like this: if God the Father did not always have God the Son, He could not have eternally been the Father. The Arians may have chanted "once Jesus was not," only to be met by Alexander's slogan, "Always Father, Always Son."[5]

Nowadays, we think about scholarly clerics as civilized men who like to wear tweed jackets and bowties and want to argue about the indigestion of angels. But in Alexandria, Egypt, in the 4th century, these theologians and pastors were the take-no-prisoner, punch-you-in-the gut, and burn-the-house down kind of people—well, at least their followers were. It makes the battling Baptists look docile in comparison. When the contention between Arius and Alexander began to spread throughout the city, it would not only cause endless debates among the citizens, but it caused riots and fighting in the streets.[6]

CONSTANTINE'S INTERVENTION

The rift in Alexandria between Arius and Bishop Alexander created a ripple effect that had massive implications for the Roman emperor, Constantine (A.D. 272-337). Constantine had come to faith in Christ purportedly because of a mystical experience he had on the eve of the Battle of Milvian Bridge in the fall of A.D. 312. Leading up to the battle, Rome had been divided between Constantine and Maxentius for nearly a decade. The two would meet on October 28th in an epic battle that would decide the fate of the empire.

On the night before the conflict, Constantine alleged to having a dream about the sun (which is the symbol of *Sol Invictus*, a Roman god that was venerated by Constantine); emblazoned over the sun was a crucifix with the words "in this sign conquer."[7] Constantine took it as a divine emblem of the Christian God's favor to be upon him in the battle. At the end of the fighting, Maxentitus lay dead, and Constantine stood victorious. Constantine then converts to Christianity and announces in A.D. 313 that Christians would no longer suffer under governmental repression.[8] Christendom, no longer pestered by the state, grew to become the official religion of Rome.

Constantine, concerned that his kingdom could once more be divided due to the doctrinal drift in A.D. 306, decided to act and bring the leading bishops, pastors, and theologians from all corners of the empire to debate and find consensus about the nature of Jesus. Many of these church leaders bore the scars of the Diocletian persecutions, some were missing eyes and others missing hands. Prior to Constantine's reforms, Christianity was outlawed, and thousands suffered as a result. For those 4th century Christians, the truth of Scripture was serious. They each paid a cost for following Jesus. Perhaps that's why some of them were so zealously militant to contend for the faith.

The bishops gathered during the summer of A.D. 325 for what has become known as *The First Council of Nicaea*. Nicaea was in the northwest region of Bithynia (today it is known as İznik, Turkey). Over 300 bishops were in attendance. They debated for three months. Though the council's agenda dealt with a wide range of matters, Alister McGrath points out that "the primary concern of the council was to formulate the identity of Jesus of Nazareth in terms that all regarded as acceptable."[9] Among those in attendance was the emperor Constantine himself. Some historians have even pointed out that the emperor took part in the debate and was active in implementing the advisement of the council.[10] Constantine's opening address to the bishops was an exhortation to find a solution. Addressing them in Latin, he said: "...begin from this moment to discard the causes of disunion which has existed among you, and remove the perplexities of controversy by embracing principles of peace."[11]

The council deliberated from late May to the end of June; all sides were considered as the theological spectrum became discernable. Although Arius was given a platform to espouse his views, they did not find favor with the council and were widely condemned by most of the bishops, with only a few dissenters. The historical figure, Saint Nicholas (known to us as the mythical figure Santa Claus) was present for the deliberations. Interestingly, Nicholas received a reprimand for laying his hands on Arius.[12] Santa found himself on Nicaea's naughty list.

NICEA'S CONCLUSIONS
Jesus is not Similar to God, Jesus is the Same as God

In the end, the council landed squarely in the camp of Bishop Alexander. Subsequently, they drafted a statement of faith that aimed at combatting Arius' teaching. In the face of heresy, the council codified what they believed in *The Nicene Creed*. The creed stated that Christ is "of the same substance of the Father, God of God, Light of Light, true God of true God, begotten not made, consubstantial with the Father." Theologian Wayne Grudem, explains:

> For all the texts that say Christ was God's 'only begotten Son' the early church felt so strongly by the force of many other texts showing that Christ was fully and completely God, that it concluded that, whatever 'only begotten' meant, it did not mean 'created.'"[13]

The key phrase being that Jesus is "of the same substance of the Father." That phrase was the crushing blow to the Arius and his followers.

The results from the council would have long-lasting implications for the church moving forward as there would be more councils to follow. Councils that would decide other crucial doctrinal issues like the nature of Christ, the nature of the Trinity, and the nature of the Holy Spirit. Overwhelmingly, the church affirmed what John said in his prologue, "In the beginning was the word, and the word was with God, and the Word was God. He was in the beginning with God (Jn 1:1-2). Jesus is not less than God and more than man; Jesus is God and man in one person.

Arianism is Outlawed

The Nicene Creed not only refuted Arius' doctrines but also issued the following judgment to those who sought to subvert the council's decision, expressing, "But for those who say, 'there was a time when he did not exist' and 'before being begotten he did not exist,' and that he came into being from non-existence, or who allege that the Son is of another *hypostasis* or *ousia*, or is alterable or changeable, these the Catholic and Apostolic church condemns."[14] Imagine using that language on your cross-embossed-paisley-*Hallmark* stationery? It does not warm the heart, but the church was right in rendering such a harsh tone. Arius may have had good intentions, but as the saying goes, "the road to hell is paved with good intentions." In A.D. 325, Arianism was condemned as heresy by the church. Arius himself was driven into exile. The wolfish theology of Arius would not, however, remain in the wilderness for long.

DON'T CALL IT A COMEBACK
Under an Arian Rule

Arianism did not go gentle into that good night—far from it. Every time you thought Arianism was dead, it showed up and wreaked almost as much havoc as before. Bishop Alexander passed away in A.D. 328 and his spiritual son, Athanasius, became the new bishop of Alexandria. Athanasius would be the one to contend against the Arians for the next 40 years. Arius may have been condemned as a heretic in A.D. 325, but he had friends in high places; friends that would wield such influence that the Nicene Creed was largely ignored for many decades. By the middle of the 4th century, as historian Jerome put it, "The whole world groaned and was astonished to find itself Arian."[15]

However, Athanasius would become known as "the father of orthodoxy," as he would spend the rest of his life contending for Nicene Christianity, but it came at a stiff price. The government, in A.D. 350, complicit with pro-Arian politicians, attempted to arrest Athanasius on trumped-up charges of murder and black magic, but he narrowly escaped. Exiled five times, Athanasius would be prolific in his writing, thus making good use of his banishments—but his health suffered immensely.[16] Despite the hardships he endured, he was able to write several works that focused on defending God-man Christianity as well as writing a critique of his opponents entitled *The Discourse*.

Arianism could have won the day had it not been for Athanasius' righteous stubbornness. At a high cost to himself, Athanasius stood against the world for the sake of championing the biblical doctrine of the deity of Christ. Unfortunately, Athanasius would not live to see the defeat of Arianism. From the time Athanasius was a teenager to the day of his death, he was mired in the theological battle that would cement some of the most crucial doctrines of Christianity. These doctrines are ancient, but they remain at the heart and soul of the Christian Gospel. They also continue to help the church differentiate between the wolves and the sheep.

LESSONS IN WOLFOLOGY

1. THE CHURCH MUST ALWAYS BE VIGILANT IN DEFENSE OF CHRISTIANITY AGAINST FALSE TEACHERS.

One side of me thinks that it is crazy to come to blows over theology. However, the other side of me thinks there is a zeal present in the ancient bishops that is missing today. Now, I am not saying that Christians today should get into physical altercations over biblical truth (although I have seen a few church league basketball games that remind me of such brutality). Still, I think that the church in the Evangelical West needs to recognize that Scripture commands us to "contend for the faith that has been once for all been delivered to the saints (Jude v 3)." That means there are times when we must be stubbornly righteous like Athanasius, and not capitulate to false teachings from within or from without.

2. DOCTRINAL CLARITY IS NOT OPTIONAL FOR THE CHURCH, IT IS INDISPENSABLE.

Believers cannot be empty-headed or nonchalant about what we believe about God, Christ, and the Gospels. We want to measure twice and cut once when it comes to our biblical doctrines. That means we must use the brain that God gave us and make it pliable to the study of Scripture and to the study of theology. We should make it our aim to, with all intellectual and spiritual power, articulate the teachings of the Scripture.

3. HERESY THRIVES UNLESS THERE ARE DOCTRINAL BOUNDARIES.

One thing we can say about the early church is that it was a wild-west frontier in terms of doctrinal conformity. A lack of doctrinal conformity creates an opportunity for heresy to make its way into the church. This is where a doctrinal statement, a summary of Christian teaching, helps us from falling into the popular heresies of our own day and time.

For example, the movie *The Shack* was popularized several years ago. Many Christians and churches supported and advocated for the book and the film—but regardless if the book is a work of fiction or not, it teaches a Trinitarian heresy known as Modalism. The fact that the broader Christian culture so greatly endorsed the book should raise legitimate concerns about the lack of biblical and doctrinal discernment in the evangelical culture of North America.

4. SOMETIMES, YOU HAVE TO STAND FOR BIBLICAL TRUTH ALONE.

Christians need to be more familiar with their history. We should read about the early martyrs, those who would not yield to the worship of Caesar—so they were crucified upside down or fed to the lions like faithful Polycarp. I would encourage believers to go and read about Martin Luther who stood against all of Rome and under the condemnation of the Papacy; or about Hugh Latimer and Nicholas Ridley who were burned to death as they took their stand against Queen Mary's attempts to stamp out English Protestantism. You can also read about Athanasius, who was exiled five times as a theological outlaw; threatened with arrest; his reputation was sullied by lies that could have gotten him executed by the Roman government.

It is my observation that there are some Christians who want to make anything and everything a hill to die on. You probably know the type: they want to argue about their pet doctrine all the time, or they always have a criticism that they cannot wait to give to a Christian leader, or they are social media zealots who call anyone who is to the left or right of them heretics. But then, there is another kind of Christian as well. The kind who doesn't think that there are any hills to die on. For Athanasius, contending for the deity of Christ was his hill. Believers today need to learn from his example, that sometimes we will have to be the ones to step up and proclaim the truth of the Gospel even if nobody else does.

5. THE DEITY OF CHRIST IS CRUCIAL TO OUR UNDERSTANDING OF THE GOSPEL.

I think if we are to understand anything about the importance of the Nicene Creed, it is that it places an exclamation point on why Jesus's deity matters. Consider why the deity of Christ matters to the centrality of the Gospel:

A. First, the Divine Nature of Christ matters because the Bible Teaches It.

At the end of the day, believers want to land where the Scriptures land. The modern Jehovah's Witnesses and Mainline Protestant Liberalism are on the opposite sides of the spectrum in terms of the outcome of their lives and their beliefs. Still, they find commonality with the Arians by denying the deity of Jesus. The true Christian says of Jesus, like Thomas before us, "My Lord and my God (Jn 20:28)."

B. Second, the Divine Nature of Christ matters because it Teaches us that God is for Us.

Despite the old Bette Midler hit, God is not watching us from a distance nor is He uninvolved in the lives of His creatures. Christ, who was eternally above us, became man to come alongside us, to redeem us at the cross. Love came down to us in Christ. God is for us. And if God is for us, who can be against us (Rom 8:31)?

C. Third, the Divine Nature of Christ matters because it reminds us that God's Ways are not Our Ways.

Every year, when Christmas rolls around, I enjoy listening to the song, "*A Strange Way to Save the World.*" It is a song that tells the story of the befuddlement of Joseph, Jesus's step-father, and his astonishment that the incarnation was God's plan to redeem fallen humanity. The lyrics express this by saying from the mouth of Joseph:

Now, I'm not one to second guess
What angels have to say
But this is such a strange
Way to save the world [17]

The song brings up a good point. There could have been an infinite number of ways for the Lord to save the world, but sending the Second person of the Trinity to become incarnate was the wisest and best way of all (1 Cor. 1:24). Arianism attempted to usurp the wisdom of God and obscure the glory of redemption by relegating Jesus to being a mere creature. Fortunately, in God's good providence, we had godly watchmen. They were willing to stand toe-to-toe with heresy to defend the Christian faith, and at times they had to do it all alone. We need more believers to be like Alexander and Athanasius, shepherds who know how to defend the sheep from the wolves.

THE NICENE CREED (A.D. 325)

We believe in one God, the Father almighty, maker of heaven and earth, of all things visible and invisible.

And in one Lord Jesus Christ, the only Son of God, begotten from the Father before all ages, God from God, Light from Light, true God from true God, begotten, not made; of the same essence as the Father. Through him all things were made. For us and for our salvation he came down from heaven; he became incarnate by the Holy Spirit and the virgin Mary, and was made human. He was crucified for us under Pontius Pilate; he suffered and was buried. The third day he rose again, according to the Scriptures. He ascended to heaven and is seated at the right hand of the Father. He will come again with glory to judge the living and the dead. His kingdom will never end.

And we believe in the Holy Spirit, the Lord, the giver of life. He proceeds from the Father and the Son, and with the Father and the Son is worshiped and glorified. He spoke through the prophets. We believe in one holy Christian[18] and apostolic church. We affirm one baptism for the forgiveness of sins. We look forward to the resurrection of the dead, and to life in the world to come. Amen.

The fact that God has become man, indeed flesh, proves that the redemption and Resurrection of the entire earthly world is not just a possibility but a reality.

—Irenaeus of Lyons, *Against Heresies*

Gnosticism

"Is there a way to encourage particular heresies?" I had to do a double take of what I just read. I realized soon enough that I was on a website that was talking about a digital strategy game set in medieval times where you not only deal with kings and queens, crusades and battles, but also popes and antipopes (this is my kind of competition). The creators designed a function into the game where heresy plays a part in defeating your opponents. Division works, even in a simulated universe. However, Christians for the past 2,000 years have not needed a video game to explain the devastation of heresy. After all, heresy is orthodoxy's evil shadow. Present, but slightly distant; not always overt, but lurking in the dark. Gnosticism is sort of like that.

Arianism is crystal clear in what it is trying to accomplish, like a straight blade that slashes right where it wants to land. However, Gnosticism is like birdshot through a 12-gauge shotgun; it sprays wide and lands all over the place, because Gnosticism is such a wide-web of beliefs. It is harder to trace than many of the other significant heresies like Arianism, Sabellianism, and Apollinarianism. In other words, delineating and discerning the nature of Gnosticism is like trying to nail Jell-O to a wall. Gnosticism is one of the oldest heresies that Christianity had to contend against. Yet, it remains relevant to esoteric spirituality embraced by many in both Eastern (Mysticism) and Western (New Age) cultures.

GNOSTICISM'S NATURE
Definition

Gnosticism, according to Everett Ferguson, is a religious movement "characterized by an intuitive knowledge of the origin, essence, and ultimate destiny of the spiritual nature of human beings."[1] The term gnostic derives from the Greek word *gnosis*, which means knowledge. Referred to as the *knowing ones*, the Gnostics planted their seeds in first century Christendom, and it began to bloom in the garden of apostolic Christianity. More technically defined, Gnosticism is:

> a complex group of movements that opposed sound doctrines. Central tenets: (1) a secret knowledge is only for elite members; (2) spiritual realities are inherently good, while physical realities are intrinsically evil; (3) thus, the Son of God could not become incarnate (embodied) by taking on material human nature (a body); (4) therefore, Jesus only appeared to be a man (Docetism).[2]

Gnosticism is concerned with escaping the soul's imprisonment in the physical body. The way to salvation is to come to true enlightenment through "secret knowledge" of the true nature of "self."

Cosmology

Gnosticism's foundational beliefs begin with a complex hierarchical structure of deities as a way of explaining the world's origins. The origin of our physical world, according to Gnosticism, is a divine accident. The divine originator (*Monad* or *The One*) created a whole stratosphere of divine entities that exist in upper and lower categories. In this structure of deities emerges goddess *Sophia* (wisdom). Sophia was to be the final emanation of the gods, which put Sophia at the terminal of the Pleroma (the heavenly realm of the gods; cf. illustration 2.1).

However, Sophia, desiring to know Monad, needed a way to break into the upper strata of Pleroma, so she recklessly begat *Demiurge* (a semi-divine) without her spouse. The result is that Demiurge is brought into existence both malformed and ignorant; thus, Demiurge is matter without spirit. Likewise, Demiurge "mistakenly believes himself to be the only god," unaware of the heavens and deities above him (closing off the ultimate reality of Pleroma).[3] Next, Demiurge crafts the material world that humans inhabit. Still, the physical world is miserable because the divine spark of man is trapped in the limitations of the physical body, enslaved to the weaknesses of human flesh, like suffering, pain, and indignity. Furthermore, humanity is an afterthought in this whole celestial drama, consigned to eternal misery unless a savior comes. Dualism emerges in this system, as a battle of the spiritual realm against the physical realm.

The Gnostic Conception of Christ

Gnosticism parasitically attached itself to first-century Christianity. Reading through Paul's letter to Colossae or the apostle John's first epistle, it is not hard to read out of those texts a discernable threat to apostolic teaching, much of it resembling Gnosticism or its cousin Docetism (the denial of Jesus's humanity). Jesus, within the scheme of Gnosticism, was an Aeon (a semi-divine, sort of like an angel) sent to bring secret knowledge to those who have been blinded and imprisoned by the physical body. Jesus, according to the Gnostic myths, broke through the veil of the material world to bring salvation to human souls that have been trapped by the physical body.

See the illustration on the next page ...

ILLUSTRATION 2.1

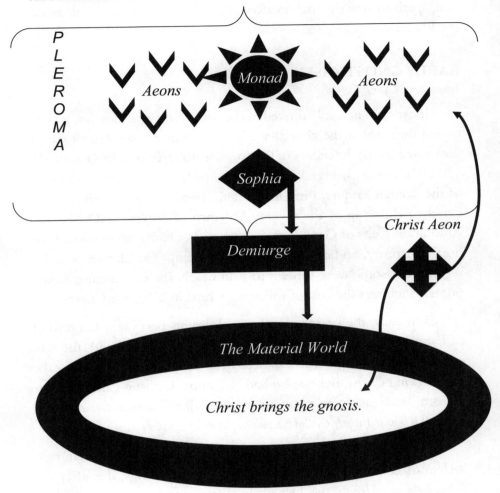

In the Gnostic conception of Jesus, "the Gnostic-Christ" operates as a spiritual coach for humanity—helping mankind find their inner light and transcend the limitations of their physical body. However, Christianity brings a different set of teachings, namely that Christ has come to save sinners from the consequences of their sins. In contrast, Gnosticism teaches that Christ has come to save people from their ignorance about the true nature of self and the true nature of reality. Under the Gnostic umbrella, it is only through the secret knowledge (gnosis) that Christ shares, enabling followers to get enough of the divine spark to free themselves from the prison of the body and attain the Pleroma.

EARLY GNOSTICISM
Irenaeus of Lyons

Gnosticism not only thrived in the days of the apostles, but it continued throughout the church age in various manifestations. One of the most notable defenders of Christianity was Irenaeus of Lyons (AD 130-202). Irenaeus served as the bishop of Lyons in the western part of the Roman Empire. Firm in the faith, Irenaeus grew spiritually under the mentoring of the revered Polycarp of Smyrna (AD 65-155). Among the Celts of Gaul, Irenaeus served as a Christian missionary in hostile territory. So horrifying was the contempt for Christians in the region, that some were thrown to wild beasts for entertainment purposes.[4] Such was the cost of following Christ in 2nd century Lyons.

Eventually, the persecution led to Irenaeus becoming the bishop of Lyons. As bishop, not only did Irenaeus have to deal with the task of shepherding people who had been bruised and battered for the sake of following Christ, but he also had to combat Gnostic-Christian syncretism. Irenaeus wrote a famous treatise called *The Detection and Overthrow of What is Falsely Called Knowledge*, also known as *Against Heresies*.

In *Against Heresies*, Irenaeus not only carefully lays out the Gnostic system of belief, but thoroughly refutes their teachings, one after the other. *Against Heresies* has helped theologians, polemicists, apologists, and scholars gain a better understanding of the pervasiveness of Gnostic teaching. Groups such as the Valentinians, Ophites, and Sethites were shot through with the spirituality of the Gnostics.[5] By today's standards, Gnosticism seems like the stuff of the *Marvel* Cinematic Universe; fixed with a cadre of gods and goddesses, redemption is restricted to only those who are privileged to this "inner spark" spirituality, without which they will be trapped in the tomb of the body forever; and ignorant deities that clumsily create a poor imitation of the heavens. Nevertheless, Gnosticism lives on in many modern movements today.

GNOSTICISM TODAY

The persistence of Gnosticism is akin to the movie monsters of my childhood. You knew that when Jason Voorhees, Freddy Krueger, and Michael Myers got axed in the final scene of the movie that they would most likely (depending on box office receipts) be back for another round of terror. They just couldn't stay dead, and neither could Gnosticism. Gnosticism thrived in the Roman Empire through various iterations, like Persian Gnosticism and Syrian-Egyptian Gnosticism. During the Middle Ages, Gnosticism found life in multiple European movements.

In the 19th century, Gnosticism maintained its staying power in movements like the Theosophical Society. While not a formal religion, the Theosophical Society promoted "religious universality" and the mysticism that has been present in Eastern religions for thousands of years.[6] Gnostic-Hermeticism had entrenched itself into popular occultism that was at work within both folk-religion, the Freemasons, and especially among the intellectual elites.

In the early 20th century, the famous British occultist Allister Crowley revived the "Gnostic Mass" and perpetuated the sexual rituals that accompanied its celebration.[7] In the realm of psychology, Carl Jung popularized major Gnostic concepts in his understanding of the human psyche.[8] Jung even paid Gnosticism a high compliment when he said, "My whole life, I have worked to know the soul and these people [Gnostics] already knew it."[9]

In 1945, the *Nag Hammadi Library* was discovered in Egypt, which enriched the modern understanding of the utility of ancient Gnostic practices. In 1958, Hans Jonas presented Gnosticism among the academics in his book *The Gnostic Religion* as a brand of existentialism that could help free people from the despair of Nihilism.[10] After World War II, Gnosticism revived itself in the form of the New Age movement.

It arrived in the United States and was pervasive in movements like Scientology, the Unification Church, and Neo-Paganism.

The New Age movement, born in the counter-culture movement of the 1960s, gave a new landscape for Neo-Gnosticism to thrive. Throughout the 1970s and 1980s, New Age Gnostic concepts of man's divine inner spark (mysticism), that all is one (monism) and all is god (pantheism), had become mainstream. Books like Ram Dass' *Be Here Now* (1971) brought Eastern mysticism into the homes of Baby Boomers. New Age esotericism even made its way into the White House when First Lady Nancy Reagan turned to astrologer Joan Quigley for numinous guidance concerning her husband's presidency.[11]

The cinematic arts gave a visual expression of Gnostic cosmic dualism in *Star Wars* (1977), which told the story of mythical energy called "the Force," that had both a light side (Jedi) and dark side (Sith); where the most spiritually enlightened could free themselves from the body and become force-ghosts. Likewise, *The Matrix* trilogy focuses on a world that has been trapped by a soulless machine that has blinded humanity with ignorance through a simulated reality. Neo, the Gnostic Christ figure, awakens to the true nature of reality by swallowing a "red pill." After acquiring this knowledge, Neo discovers his unlimited potential and leverages it to successfully make war against the machine. In the final scene, Neo threatens the mechanistic system, stating:

> I don't know the future. I didn't come here to tell you how this is going to end. I came here to tell you how it's going to begin. I'm going to hang up this phone, and then I'm going to show these people what you don't want them to see. I'm going to show them a world without you, a world without rules and controls, without borders or boundaries, a world where anything is possible.[12]

Dan Brown's *The Da Vinci Code* (a major pop-culture success in both books and movies) uses central ideas found in the *Gnostic Gospels* that deny both Nicene orthodoxy and that Christ is the savior who has come to atone for sins. For Brown, Jesus is a guru who has only come to enlighten people with knowledge.[13]

More recently, Gnostic principles have been popularized by the likes of Deepak Chopra and Eckhart Tolle. For example, Tolle said in his book *The New Earth* (2005) that Jesus is simply a "light" to help humankind attain their highest potential.[14] The implication is that man suffers from a form of blindness, causing them to walk in darkness. But this darkness is not sin, rather it is the need for "the light of consciousness," that Christ (and other spiritual leaders) has come to share.[15] Chopra explains in his bestselling book *The Seven Laws of Spiritual Success* (1994) that "we are divinity in disguise, and the gods and goddesses in embryo that are contained within us seek to be fully materialized. True success is, therefore, the experience of the miraculous. It is the unfolding of divinity within us."[16]

From the 1st century apostolic church to the silver screen of Hollywood, Gnosticism continues to cast a wide net. It may seem that as the broader culture becomes more secularized, it buys into materialism and rejects issues pertaining to the soul. However, it is just not true. As the culture becomes more secular, it becomes more spiritual. Sadly, it is not Christian spirituality. Instead, it is Modern Pagan and Neo-Gnostic spirituality manifested in movements like Wicca, Spiritism, and Esoteric-Occultism. In the United States, even as the dam of nominal Christianity has collapsed over the past 50 years, the spirituality of people in the West continues with misguided fervor.

LESSONS IN WOLFOLOGY

1. IGNORANCE IS NOT MAN'S FUNDAMENTAL PROBLEM: SIN IS.

Scripture teaches that man has been corrupted by the original sin of our first parents in the Garden (Gen 3:1-6; Rom 5:12-14). The cause of our physical and spiritual death is rooted in the inherited guilt of Adam and Eve as well as the sin that we willfully choose to do (Ps 51:5; Rom 6:23). Our minds have been corrupted by the damage wrought by sin (*the noetic effects of sin*). Paul explains, "In their case [unbelievers] the god of this world [Satan] has blinded the minds of the unbelievers, to keep them from seeing the light of the gospel of the glory of Christ, who is the image of God (2 Cor 4:4)."

Human sin is an act of "cosmic treason" against God, which is why it deserves the harshest of penalties, meted out in an eternity of Hell.[17] The only hope humanity has is found in Jesus, who has come from heaven not simply to enlighten man, so that they might fulfill their potential, but to save them from the consequences of God's judgment. Christ has come to bring sinful man back from the pigpens of despair into the Father's house (Lk 15:11-32). Today, many well-intentioned people believe gun violence, injustice, sex trafficking, and terrorism can be undone by cutting through the ignorance of humanity, as though education and legislation turn the tide of man's heart. Such a mentality proves just how naïve people can be.

Anyone who adopts the biblical view of humanity's total depravity will see quickly that man's greatest problem is his rebellion against a Holy God. The good news of the Gospel is not that we have an enlightened teacher, but a prophet, high priest, and a king who bled and died for our redemption (Ps 2:1-12; Heb 1:1-3; Acts 2:30-33; 1 Jn 2:1).

2. THE HUMAN BODY IS NOT A TOMB TO ESCAPE FROM, BUT A TEMPLE FOR THE HOLY SPIRIT TO DWELL IN.

Gnosticism's entire premise is that the body is a trap, a divine accident, that now imprisons the soul. It is not hard to understand why some could think this way. After all, the body gets sick, gets tired, and ages. If you trip, you can fall and break bones. If you are not careful with a knife, you could lose a finger. It seems like there is a future price to pay for all the bumps we have taken in the past. The body is weak, but it is not a tomb.

The Scriptures teach us that humanity bears the image of God (1:27). God created man, with body and soul, to display His divine imprint upon us. In other words, human life is incredibly valuable. Just consider all the times the Lord emphasizes so many prohibitions against the taking of life and the shedding of blood (Gen 9:6; Ex 20:13;

Dt 19:10, 27:24; 1st Sam 19:5; Pro 6:16-19). The human body is precious to God—*life is in our blood* (Lev 17:11). Our very form, according to Scripture, is by the craftsmanship of God's hand. The Psalmist tells us, "For you formed my inward parts; you knitted me together in my mother's womb. I praise you, for I am fearfully and wonderfully made. Wonderful are your works; my soul knows it very well (Ps 139:13-14)." While it remains true that human sin has devastated the relationship that man has with God, God's image remains on the sinner.

Our body, comprised of flesh, blood, and bone, is a gift from God to us. The body is not primarily for our own amusement; instead, the body is to be consecrated to God as a living sacrifice of praise (Rom 12:1-2). Paul mentions the danger of believers in Corinth joining themselves to the myriad of prostitutes in the red-light district of town; he writes:

> Flee from sexual immorality. Every other sin a person commits is outside the body, but the sexually immoral person sins against his own body. Or do you not know that your body is a temple of the Holy Spirit within you, whom you have from God? You are not your own, for you were bought with a price. So glorify God in your body (1 Cor 5:18-19).

The human frame is sacred precisely because the Spirit of God dwells inside the believer. This means, that believers should honor the Lord by not abusing it (through drugs, alcohol, or gluttony) or misusing it (through sexual immorality). In short, God cares about the human body, and so should we.

3. THE MATERIAL WORLD IS NOT A COSMIC MISTAKE BUT A CAREFUL DESIGN.

The Gnostic cosmology is a story about a jaded goddess who desired to rise above her station and ascend to the One. In a tizzy, Sophia begat Demiurge; and then Demiurge, the semi-divine-red-neck-troglodyte, mistakenly begat our universe. This sounds like a plot to a Monty Python film. Nevertheless, it is clear from both nature and Scripture that the universe God made exists intentionally and for His good purposes (Pro 21:1; Is 10:5-7; Dan 2:31-38). Likewise, God sovereignly governs all that takes place and unfolds history by His providence (Rom 8:28; Phil 4:19; Mt 6:26).

Paul explains that God's "invisible attributes, namely, his eternal power and divine nature, have been clearly perceived, ever since the creation of the world, in the things that have been made (Rom 1:20)." Creation is not a can of paint that accidentally got kicked over and thrown down the cosmic corridors of the heavens. Instead, the created universe operates and functions with symmetry and precision, with no end to its complexities. Consider the majesty of a school of angelfish parading through the turquoise blue Caribbean Sea, or the peculiar design of the translucent Amber Phantom butterfly; or the sheer wonder of the *Pillars of Creation* in the Eagle Nebulae.

The physical world we inhabit is not a disastrous mistake; instead, it is a meticulous design.

4. THE FUTURE STATE OF THE BELIEVER IS NOT A DISEMBODIED SOUL, BUT A SOUL THAT HAS BEEN REUNITED WITH OUR RESURRECTED BODY.

I have been involved in end-of-life-ministry for many years. I have had several conversations with people who suffered from terrible diseases, like pancreatic cancer, Parkinson's, and COPD. One thing that has always concerned me is how many of them were professing Christians, and yet they would say things like, "I can't wait to be freed from this body and be with the Lord." Now, on the one hand, I can appreciate what they are saying. Nobody wants to suffer from the pains that are associated with death. Likewise, the Bible does tell us that "we would rather be away from the body and at home with the Lord (2 Cor 5:8)." On the other hand, I was discerning from these types of discussions that there was a subtle Gnostic tendency at work to reject the physical body in favor of the "superior" spiritual realm.

However, the Christian hope is for our souls to be restored to our resurrected and glorified bodies in the New Heavens and New Earth with Christ (Rev 20:4-6, 11-13; 21:1-4). As Christ was raised on the third day, so too will Christians be raised on the Day of the Lord. The

Christian hope is not to be a disembodied soul under the altar of God for eternity. Instead, the Christian hope is to have body and soul reunited in the Resurrection (1ˢᵗ Cor 15:42-49) and to dwell physically in the presence of Christ forever (1 Cor 13:12; Rev 19:9).

5. JESUS IS NOT A GHOST OR A SPIRIT, JESUS IS FULLY MAN AND FULLY GOD.

It cannot be stressed enough: if you are looking for a grid that will explain a cohesive and monolithic Gnostic worldview you will end up being frustrated. Gnosticism is a web that is strewn in many different directions, and so there is a lot of variation. Nonetheless, Douglas Groothius gives the following insight: "Although Gnostic teachings show some diversity on this subject, they tend toward Docetism—the doctrine that the descent of the Christ was spiritual and not material, despite any *appearance* of materiality."[18] In other words, Gnosticism usually subscribes to the view that Jesus was immaterial (a ghost, a spirit, or an angel), in opposition to the apostolic writings that place a strong emphasis upon the physical nature of Jesus.

As soon as you open a copy of the Scriptures and turn to the Gospels, they point us to the supernatural birth of Christ that took place in the natural human way. Conceived by the Holy Spirit and born of the virgin Mary, Jesus enters our world through the stables of Bethlehem (Lk 1:26-35; 2:1-7; Mt 1:18-24). Anyone who has been present for the birth of a child understands that it is a viscerally human experience filled with blood, sweat, and tears (of pain and joy).

Jesus goes through all the stages of human development and the process of learning (Lk 2:52). In His passion, we see that Christ suffers from the whip, the crown of thorns, and the nails in His hands and feet (Lk 22:63-23:49; Mk 14:43-65; Jn 18:1-19:34). When Thomas rejects the apostles' testimony that Jesus has been physically raised—he demands proof, declaring, "Unless I see in his hands the mark of the nails, and place my finger into the mark of the nails, and place my hand into his side, I will never believe (Jn 20:25)." We then see that sometimes the Lord gives us the evidence we ask for, as Jesus tells Thomas,

"Put your finger here, and see my hands; and put out your hand, and place it in my side. Do not disbelieve, but believe (Jn 20:27)."

John opens his first epistle by emphasizing the corporeal nature of Christ's incarnation, writing, "That which was from the beginning, which we have heard, which we have seen with our eyes, which we looked upon and have touched with our hands, concerning the word of life (1 Jn 1:1)." Jesus was born "under the law" and "in the likeness of man" to redeem us from "the curse of the law (Gal 3:13; 4:4; Phil 2:7)." Christians have a savior who is a true person, a fully human man that we desire to spend eternity with. This man is Jesus. Jesus is not a ghost, or a spirit, or a celestial enlightener—Jesus is the second person of the Trinity (fully God) who took on human flesh (fully Man) to save His people from their sins (Mt 1:21). The Heidelberg Catechism explains the importance of Christ's nature by saying that humanity needs a mediator "who is true and righteous human, yet more powerful than all creatures, that is, one who is also true God."[19] Jesus is no angel. Jesus is not a ghost. Jesus is God in human flesh.

THE CHALCEDONIC DEFINITION (A.D. 425)

Therefore, following the holy fathers, we all with one accord teach men to acknowledge one and the same Son, our Lord Jesus Christ, at once complete in Godhead and complete in manhood, truly God and truly man, consisting also of a reasonable soul and body; of one substance with the Father as regards his Godhead, and at the same time of one substance with us as regards his manhood; like us in all respects, apart from sin; as regards his Godhead, begotten of the Father before the ages, but yet as regards his manhood begotten, for us men and for our salvation, of Mary the Virgin, the God-bearer; one and the same Christ, Son, Lord, Only-begotten, recognized in two natures, without confusion, without change, without division, without separation; the distinction of natures being in no way annulled by the union, but rather the characteristics of each nature being preserved and coming together to form one person and subsistence, not as parted or separated into two persons, but one and the same Son and Only-begotten God the Word, Lord Jesus Christ; even as the prophets from earliest times spoke of him, and our Lord Jesus Christ himself taught us, and the creed of the fathers has handed down to us.

Beloved, although I was very eager to write to you about our common salvation, I found it necessary to write appealing to you to contend for the faith that was once for all delivered to the saints.

—Jude, v 3

Modalism/Sabellianism

There were times in my teenage years when I thought algebra was detrimental to my health. Given some of the complexities of certain equations, I thought to myself that it would not be long until my brain turned into a puddle of lukewarm gray soup. But difficult problems are a part of life. People face all kinds of challenges, like understanding molecular biology, or rebuilding a transmission, or coaching pee-wee soccer (to each his own). The same holds true in the realm of Christian theology. Though it is tempting, not everything in Christianity can be reduced to *"What would Jesus do?"* There are complicated components to Christian theology, especially in the study of the Godhead.

Early Christianity had to theologically mine the apostolic teachings they received, while at the same time combating heresy that invaded the church. In other words, Christianity's understanding of the nature of the Godhead and the nature of Jesus (Christology) took time to figure out. During the developmental stages of early Christianity, there were trials and errors.

However, that does not mean that the ecumenical church councils were doctrinal factories, as though they were creating new dogma and sending it down the assembly line of theological ideas. What they were doing was using the biblical data to frame up the church's fundamental doctrines with the most exact terminology possible. Still, determining how to define the nature of The Godhead was one of the most perplexing challenges of the patristic church.

SEEDS OF SABELIANISM

Prior to the ecumenical councils of the patristic era (Nicaea, Chalcedon) the church did not articulate, with any consensus, the precise nature of The Godhead. This created theological quandaries for pastors and teachers who were on a quest to communicate, to the best of their abilities and intellect, what the Scriptures teach concerning the nature of God. Several false teachers throughout the history of the church attempted to resolve theological knots but ended up breaking the string altogether. Then things really got messy.

Dynamic Monarchianism / Adoptionism

Dynamic Monarchianism, otherwise known as *Adoptionism*, is ultimately a Christological heresy. However, it has negative consequences for a proper understanding of the Christian Godhead too. The first platform that developed for the Adoptionist movement came from a Jewish-Christian sect known as the *Ebionites*.

The Ebionites emerged in the 2nd century as a movement that was stalwart in their defense of the oneness of God. The primary issue is that they failed "to do justice the full significance of Jesus of Nazareth."[1] Like Arianism before it, the Ebionites reduced Jesus to the status of a mere a prophet. The Ebionites viewed Jesus as a natural man, who by his efforts, attained exaltation to divine status.

Another Adoptionist perspective arose in Rome in A.D. 190 through the teachings of Theodotus the Tanner.[2] Theodotus emphasized that Christ was only human (psilanthropist) and became adopted by God at his baptism (Mt 3:13-17). In the views espoused by Theodotus, Jesus was not the Logos that existed co-eternally with God; instead, Jesus was a mere man that received his deity by way of adoption. Into the 3rd century, a leading teacher, Paul of Samosata, expanded upon Theodotus's views. Paul reiterated that Jesus could maintain "constant union with God" because of the moral perfection that Christ exhibited through his obedience.[3] However, Paul's views were condemned by church leadership at the Synod of Antioch in A.D. 268.[4]

SABBELLIANISM IN FULL BLOOM
Modalistic Monarchianism

Millard Erickson defines Modalistic Monarchianism as "A movement that interpreted the Trinity as successive revelations of God—first as Father, then as Son, and finally as Holy Spirit."[5] This view knocks out the pillars of distinctions between the divine beings, which collapses the Godhead into a singularity. In other words, for Modalistic Monarchianism, there is only one God, which means "the Father and the Son were different expressions of the same being."[6]

In the Modalistic scheme, the roles that God played were predicated upon the actions He takes in history. For example,

> When God acts as a creator, we [Modalists] understand him as God the Father. When he acts as the redeemer, we understand him as God the Son. When he acts as a sanctifier, we understand him as God the Holy Spirit. There are no distinct persons in the Trinity or any kind of change.[7]

Modalism is as appealing as it is dangerous. The alluring aspect of Modalism is that it makes the nature of God easier to understand and simpler to explain.

A major advocate for Modalism was an early 3rd century teacher named Praxeas. Little is known about Praxeas, but the church father Tertullian wrote a whole treatise entitled *Against Praxeas* (not as cool as *Wolfology*, but probably better) as a way of contradicting the movement's fundamental ideas. Chief among them was *patripassianism.* Patripassianism is the perspective that it was God the Father who died as the Son, on the Cross. The logic is not hard to understand; in Modalism, God is one without distinct personhoods.

The oneness of God means that there is no difference between God the Father and God the Son, for they are the same; the Father, acting as the Son, endures the agony of Golgotha. Thus, Modalistic Monarchianism negates the particular redemptive work of Jesus in favor of maintaining God's oneness. From Tertullian's vantage point Praxeas was the devil's servant, for "he drove away prophecy, and he brought in heresy; he put to flight the Paraclete, and he crucified the Father."[8] However, Praxeas was quite convincing. The Modalism postulated by Praxeas made in-roads in Rome for a time, that is until he was excommunicated and "justly condemned by the church fathers."[9]

God's indivisibility was the chief goal of the Monarchian parties. The Adoptionists and the Modalist approached the oneness of God from different perspectives. The Adoptionists were bent on denying Jesus's deity; whereas the Modalists were primarily concerned with upholding a simple monotheism without the complexities of early Trinitarian formulas. Inevitably, Monarchianism comes to full maturity in the controversial figure of Sabellius. That there is sparse information about Sabellius (as well other historical heretics) testifies to the efforts of orthodox theologians and apologists to stamp out error where and when they found it. After all, history is usually written by the winners.

Although Sabellius is a historical footnote in early Christianity, his contributions at the time strengthened Modalism's staying power. Justin Holcomb explains:

> While early versions of Modalism stood out as simplistic and easily dismissible, Sabellius gave the teaching a facelift, making it much more advanced and defensible. In Sabellianism, Father, Son, and the Holy Spirit are just three different hats or masks that God wears, as the situation demands.[10]

Sabellius' successive understanding of the nature of God stood in conflict with those who championed proto-Trinitarianism. While some movements (like Manicheism and the Monophysites) were explicating doctrines such as ditheism (the belief in two gods) and tritheism (the belief in three gods), Sabellius was concerned with defending monotheism. Ultimately, Sabellius' views were condemned by pope Callistus in A.D. 220 and by the later ecumenical councils that followed (Nicaea, Constantinople, and Chalcedon).[11]

MODALISM POST-REFORMATION: UNITARIANISM

Anti-Trinitarian rhetoric has been at work in the church since the 2nd century. As the ecumenical councils emerged and began to codify the central tenants of the Christian faith (in *The Nicene Creed, The Definition of Chalcedon,* and *The Apostle's Creed*), those who contradicted the Trinity were marked as heretics. Fast-forward to just after the Protestant Reformation, and you see the new emergence of Anti-Trinitarianism in radical figures like Michael Servatus (1511-1553) and Fausto Socinus (1539-1604)—as well as movements like the Polish Brethren. The first Unitarian church came about during the middle 16th century in Transylvania, out of the Anabaptist radical reformation movement (cf. *The Racovian Confession*).

The name Unitarian derives from the movement's belief in the uni-personality of God, which is a repudiation of orthodox Trinitarianism. Likewise, Unitarians reject the deity of Christ and affirm the teaching of Universalism (the belief that all humanity will be saved). These ideas spread to the West. Unitarians in England emerged and gained a foothold throughout the 17th and 18th centuries. However, Britain did try to curtail the influx of the Anti-Trinitarians in the 1689 *Act of Toleration,* which allowed freedom of worship only to orthodox Christian non-conformists.

Towards the end of the 18th century, Thomas Paine's *Age of Reason* further promoted Unitarian-Deism in both the United States and England. King's Chapel in Boston, Massachusetts became the first Unitarian congregation in the 1780s under the leadership of James Freeman.[12] During the 19th century, Unitarianism in America would be popularized by the likes of William Ellery Channing and Andrews Norton.

Officially, the American Unitarian Association began in 1825 and then later merged in 1961 with the Universalist Church of America to become the Unitarian Universalist Association (UUA). The UUA is

guided by seven principles that emphasize peace, love, justice and respect towards all mankind. As a denomination, the UUA has remained
mostly stagnant since its inception in 1961. Unitarian Universalists are
the left-wing branch of Modalism.

MODERN SABELLIANISM
Oneness Pentecostalism

I was a child of the 1980s, so I caught the tail end of the Cold War.
I grew up watching movies like *The Day After* (1983) and *The Last Testament* (1983) that emphasized the horrors of nuclear war. While watching these movies, my grandfather, Grandpa Mark, would see the size
of my eyes and say, "Don't worry, Tobby. If nuclear bombs dropped,
we would hardly know it—we would be wiped out in an instant." For
some reason, this did not do a good job of comforting me (I am just
grateful that my grandfather worked in sanitation and not in suicide
prevention). Then he would say, "Cockroaches would be the only sur-
vivors of nuclear war." Cockroaches have strong staying power, and
they also play a vital role in our ecosystem (nature's bottom feeders),
but nobody wants them in their home. Heresy can be a lot like those
unwanted cockroaches—no matter what happens to it, heresy finds a
way to survive.

The modern iteration of ancient Sabellianism is found in the Oneness Pentecostal (sometimes known as "Apostolic Pentecostals" or
"Jesus Only") movement that began in the early years of the 20th century. Sabellianism is 1700 years removed from its modern successor.
So, one might wonder what the ancient form and modern form have
in common. Edward Dalcour answers that,

> Despite many Oneness teachers and advocates throughout the
> years differing on many tangential doctrines, one theological point
> is firmly agreed upon by all Oneness believers historically and pres-
> ently: God is unipersonal and has not revealed Himself in three
> distinct, coequal, coeternal, coexistent Persons or Selves.[13]

There are several Oneness Pentecostal denominations today, but it is
the United Pentecostal Church International (UPCI) that is the largest

representation of the movement. The UPCI was founded in 1945. According to its website, the UPCI boasts of over 5 million members.[14] This movement is rooted in the early 20th century Pentecostal awakening in the *Azusa Street Revival* of 1901.[15]

There are four main characteristics of Oneness Pentecostalism: first, salvation is by faith in Jesus only; second, baptism is done in Jesus's name only; third, strict external holiness standards are expected; and fourth, each member should give evidence of speaking in tongues.[16] Whereas Unitarians are the progressive movement of Modalism, Oneness Pentecostals are in the hard-right fundamentalist Modalist camp. Further, Oneness Pentecostals share a similar view of the Godhead with their ancient ancestors in that they "declare that the Godhead consists of only one person and deny the traditional doctrine of the Trinity. They maintain that the only real 'person' in the Godhead is Jesus."[17] Gregory Boyd, the author of *Oneness Pentecostals and The Trinity* (1992), explains that "Oneness groups deduce that Jesus is God in his totality, and therefore Jesus must himself be the Father, Son, and Holy Spirit. This implies, of course, that the orthodox doctrine of the Trinity…is erroneous."[18]

BAD ANALOGIES

I heard a story once about a man who began to say, "A wife is like a dog…." Nobody knows how the rest of that story goes, but the word is the man was never seen or heard from again. Bad analogies can be dangerous, especially when we are trying to communicate the nature of God in simple terminology. I remember attending Sunday School in my early twenties and well-meaning "Bible" teachers trying to communicate to the class their understanding of the Godhead and botching it in ways that would make demons laugh and angels cry. Carl Trueman wrote, "…analogies for the Trinity are unhelpful because the Trinity is absolutely unique. There is no analogy to the created world that is more helpful than it is misleading."[19]

There are two specific analogies that are referenced regarding Modalism. The first is *The Water Analogy*. The water analogy attempts to teach the Christian conception of the Godhead by stating that water (H_2O) remains water regardless if it is a solid, a liquid, or gaseous. While it is true that an ice cube, a puddle, and a plume of steam are water in three-forms, it is also true that water cannot simultaneously exist in all three states at once. Of course, what is glaring in this attempt to teach the Trinity, the water analogy ends up teaching Modalistic heresy.

Then there is *The Egg Analogy*. Just as one full egg is composed of the shell, the yoke, and the egg white, so too the Trinity is composed of God the Father, the Son, and the Holy Spirit. Sounds good, right? Likewise, you can visually illustrate this for people and etch the idea into someone's mind. Sadly, the illustration can land us back into the false teaching of Modalism. The egg is one, but it has three different elements. A yoke is different than egg white. The shell is different than a yoke. An egg white is different than a shell. I think you get the picture. However, in three concise statements, we can state the Triune nature of God:

1. God is three persons.

2. Each person is fully God.

3. There is one God.

These three statements may not be as illustrative as the water and the egg analogies, but they are accurate; likewise, they are concise and precise.

Helpful here is the Athanasian Creed, which came along in the 5th century to make some crucial distinctions about the Christian understanding of the Trinity. The language is blunt, but there is potency in the creed's summary of the doctrine concerning the nature of God and the nature of Christ. Consider this brief excerpt from *The Athanasian Creed*:

The Holy Spirit is of the Father and of the Son; neither made, nor created, nor begotten, but proceeding. So there is one Father, not three Fathers; one Son, not three Sons; one Holy Spirit, not three Holy Spirits. And in this Trinity none is afore or after another; none is greater or less than another. But the whole three persons are coeternal and coequal.[20]

Our summary of the doctrine of the Trinity is not exhaustive, but it is meant as a clarification of what the Bible reveals about God's triune nature. God has given us all the information that He wants us to know and believe about Him in His Holy Word.

LESSONS IN WOLFOLOGY

1. THE DESIRE FOR DOCTRINAL SIMPLICITY CAN SOMETIMES LEAD TO BIBLICAL INFIDELITY.

In Evangelical Christianity, we like things to be boiled down for us in simple terms. At Vacation Bible School, we expect broad biblical principles, some choreographed line dancing, snack time, and the ABC's of salvation: *Admit, Believe*, and *Confess.* We do not always put the same kind of effort in our theology that we might put into our trigonometry. That is why one of the most appealing aspects of Modalism is that it makes the nature of God easier to comprehend and easier to articulate. For Modalists, it is easier to affirm one God with three different forms than it is to affirm the one God who exists simultaneously as three persons who share the same divine nature.

Now the desire to comprehend God is good, and it is possible because of divine revelation. God has revealed all that He wants us to believe about Him in the Bible (Dt 29:29). Making sense of all the biblical data has been an arduous task that took place over hundreds of years, numerous theological controversies, and ecumenical councils to sort out. Yet Modalism is still prevalent in the world today through Oneness Pentecostalism (Fundamentalistic Modalism) and Unitarianism (Liberal Modalism). However, the real danger of modern Modalism is how it has taken a foothold in many churches because the doctrine of the Trinity is assumed, implicitly denied, or rejected out-right in favor of easier conceptions of God.

2. MODALISM REJECTS THE HEART OF THE CHRISTIAN GOSPEL—PENAL SUBSTITUTIONARY ATONEMENT.

Penal Substitutionary Atonement (PSA) is the view that the person of Jesus Christ suffered the penalty for sin on the Cross, as a substitute for sinners, and to provide a satisfactory atonement that appeases the wrath of God against sin (Jn 10:10; Rom 3:25-26; 5:6-10; Heb 9:26). But Modalism must reject this view of the atonement. The reason is that in PSA, Jesus's death satisfies God the Father's desire for justice against sin. In other words, at the Cross, there is a clear distinction of persons—God the Father (Judge) and Christ the Son (Sacrifice). Jesus cries from the Cross, "My God, my God why have you forsaken me (Mt 27:46)," denying the Sabellian teaching of patripassianism that falsely asserted that the Father suffered on the Cross as the Son.

3. THE MODALISM HERESY ARISES OUT OF A DEEPLY FLAWED INTERPRETATION OF SCRIPTURE.

Modalism swings on the hinges of an isolated interpretation of se-lect Bible passages, unaided by the guidance of the whole counsel of God's Word. So, biblical texts that articulate either the monotheistic nature of God (Dt 6:4; Is 9:6) or texts where the Bible emphasizes the unity of the Father and the Son (Mt 28:19; Jn 10:30; 14:9) are used by those in the Sabellian camp to construct their view of God. However, *the Analogy of Faith (analogia fidei)* means that we must interpret Scripture in light of Scripture.

Consider this: when Jesus tells His disciples in John 10:30 that "I and the Father are one," we have to look at the narrow context (John 10 and the Gospel of John) as well as the wider context (both the Old and New Testaments). In the narrow context of John 10, Jesus is mak-ing clear distinctions of persons (10:29; 31-38): there is Jesus the Son and God the Father. Likewise, the use of the designation of Father (*Pater*) is used 250 times in John's Gospel, which further emphasizes the distinction between the Father and the Son. Furthermore, in John 1, the text says, "In the beginning was the Word (*Logos*), and the Word was with God (*Theon*), and the Word was God." Christ is the eternal Logos and fully divine, but He is also distinct in His person, for John says, "the Word was with God."

When you take a step back from the narrow-context and begin to look at the wider context of John 10:30, you have to harmonize it with a text like Matthew 3:16-17, the depiction of Jesus's baptism that says, "And when Jesus was baptized, immediately he went up from the water, and behold, the heavens were opened to him, and he saw the Spirit of God descending like a dove and coming to rest on him; and behold, a voice from heaven said, 'This is my beloved Son, with whom I am well pleased.'" At Jesus's baptism, we have a fuller picture of the distinct personhood of the one God: the satisfied Father, the obedient Son, and the protector—the Holy Spirit.[21] Likewise, the Old Testament emphasizes a plurality in the Godhead (Gen 1:26; 11:7; Is 6:8), which also implies the distinction of persons.

4. STAY AWAY FROM BAD ANALOGIES OF THE TRINITY AND STICK TO PRECISE SUMMARIES OF THE TRINITY INSTEAD.

In most situations, both illustrations and analogies are helpful. But regarding the Trinity, it most often leads into mischaracterization of who the Bible reports God to be. Consider the full gamut of analogies people have attempted to use to explain the Trinity: The Egg Analogy, The Water Analogy, The Relationship Analogy (husband, father, son), or The Shamrock Analogy. Each one of them, though well-intended, leads people to adopt a view that contradicts the nature of God. It is much better for believers to be precise and concise in our summary statements of the Godhead: God is three persons; each person is fully God; there is one God.

AN EXCERPT FROM
THE ATHANASIAN CREED
(5ᵀᴴ CENTURY)

But the Godhead of the Father, of the Son, and of the Holy Spirit is all one, the glory equal, the majesty coeternal. Such as the Father is, such is the Son, and such is the Holy Spirit. The Father uncreated, the Son uncreated, and the Holy Spirit uncreated. The Father incomprehensible, the Son incomprehensible, and the Holy Spirit incomprehensible. The Father eternal, the Son eternal, and the Holy Spirit eternal. And yet they are not three eternals but one eternal.

As also there are not three uncreated nor three incomprehensible, but one uncreated and one incomprehensible. So likewise, the Father is almighty, the Son almighty, and the Holy Spirit almighty. And yet they are not three almighties, but one almighty. So the Father is God, the Son is God, and the Holy Spirit is God; And yet they are not three Gods, but one God. So likewise the Father is Lord, the Son Lord, and the Holy Spirit Lord; And yet they are not three Lords but one Lord.

For like as we are compelled by the Christian verity to acknowledge every Person by himself to be God and Lord; So are we forbidden by the Christian[22] religion to say; There are three Gods or three Lords. The Father is made of none, neither created nor begotten. The Son is of the Father alone; not made nor created, but begotten. The Holy Spirit is of the Father and of the Son; neither made, nor created, nor begotten, but proceeding. So there is one Father, not three Fathers; one Son, not three Sons; one Holy Spirit, not three Holy Spirits. And in this Trinity none is afore or after another; none is greater or less than another. But the whole three persons are coeternal, and coequal. So that in all things, as aforesaid, the Unity in Trinity and the Trinity in Unity is to be worshipped.

Prologue to Chapter 4: I Have a Confession to Make

I need to make a confession. I love Mormons. Now you may read this chapter and think otherwise, but sometimes you have to wound those you love for the sake of their own good. Like that time in the movie *Speed*, when to save the hostage, a young officer played by Keanu Reeves, had to shoot the hostage in the leg. The hostage had his leg in tatters, but his life was spared. It gives a whole new meaning to "Faithful are the wounds of a friend (Prv 27:6)."

I look at Mormons as a tribe, especially those Mormons out in Utah and Idaho where it is a dense area for the Church of Jesus Christ of Latter-day Saints (LDS). I enjoy interacting with Mormon missionaries and talking to Mormons whenever and wherever I find them. My wife, Rachel, will tell you right now that if I come within 20 feet of Mormon missionaries, she will give me a peck on the cheek and tell me she will see me in two hours (that's not an exaggeration). I'm like the Dr. Seuss of Mormon engagement:

> *I will talk to a Mormon on my jog;*
> *I will talk to a Mormon in the fog.*
> *I will speak with a missionary in my house;*
> *I will speak with a missionary while I hunt a mouse.*
> *I will listen to LDS here and there;*
> *I will listen to LDS everywhere.*

However, one of the reasons I love Mormons so much is that I used to be one. My family converted to the LDS church when I was 11. I come from a long history of lapsed Roman Catholics and nominal Protestants—sort of a patchwork of spirituality that promoted gambling on one hand and guilt on the other. When my family turned to Mormonism, we had found a spiritual home for the first time. Fortunately, God's grace intervened in my life and I became a follower of the biblical Christ. I found a new home in the local Church and in historic Christian orthodoxy.

Now, I know what you're thinking, "The author has a chip on his shoulder against Mormons and cannot be objective about it." I admit that bias is probably a factor for most people, and it no doubt affects me, too; this was especially true when I first became a Christian in 1995. I was 17. I will admit it—I felt deceived. I also felt wounded by some members of my family who remain nominally affiliated with the LDS to this day. I *was* angry.

But as I grew in Christ, I realized that all Mormons are deceived (like all people without Jesus). There was nothing especially abnormal about me that brought me into the LDS church. All are sinners. According to scripture, humanity is "blinded" by the "god of this world" (2 Cor 4:4). Besides, it is not like there is a soul-eating machine deep in the underbelly of the Salt Lake Temple that feeds off the conversions of naïve rubes. Mormons believe what they believe just like anybody else. They think it is true.

Honestly, as an Evangelical Christian pastor, I am not only challenged by the zeal that Mormons have for their beliefs, but I am also concerned about the lack of evangelism on the part of my own Christian community. So, I have a lot of respect for Mormon missionaries and have encountered many lovely people over the years who are affiliated with the LDS movement. I like to think that I look at the young men (LDS Missionaries) who come to my door to share *Another Testimony of Jesus* with the eyes of a concerned father. So, this is my confession. Can I be fair in my assessments? You will have to be the judge of that.

Satan disguises himself as an angel of light. So it is no surprise if his servants, also, disguise themselves as servants of righteousness. Their end will correspond to their deeds.

—2nd Corinthians 11:14-15

Mormonism

I tell my son that 100 percent of all fights can be avoided. The best way to prevent a conflict is to simply pick an exit strategy and walk away. However, I remember being an unregenerate young boy, on the precipice of my teenage years and having schoolmates pick on one another—sometimes it was brutal. If you wanted to hurt a classmate, you would say something derogatory about their mother.

Suffice it to say, one only needs to spend a few hours with pre-teen boys to discover the doctrine of total depravity, experientially speaking. And saying something insulting about a boy's mother was probably the best way to challenge the principle that *all fights are avoidable.* Yep, if you bad-mouthed someone's mom in the group of kids I ran around with, you had better have good dental insurance—because someone was bound to get a few teeth knocked out. So, just imagine the treachery of a classmate calling your mother, your sister, or your girlfriend a prostitute? That is not a fight you can easily walk away from.

Well, that is where we start with Joseph Smith. The founder and first prophet of the LDS movement. Smith stated such words of condemnation upon the Protestant Christianity of the 19th century, when he writes, the great and abominable church [Protestants, Roman Catholics, and Greek Orthodox], which is the *whore* of all the earth, shall be cast down by devouring fire, according to as it is spoken by the mouth of Ezekiel the prophet, who spoke of these things, which have not come to pass but surely must, as I live, for abominations shall not reign.[1]

As the old-timers used to say, "Them's fighting words." Smith propagated an idea called *The Great Apostasy*. The LDS church explains through their online dictionary *True to Faith* what they mean by The Great Apostasy:

> During the Great Apostasy, people were without divine direction from living prophets. Many churches were established, but they did not have priesthood power to lead people to the true knowledge of God the Father and Jesus Christ. Parts of the holy Scriptures were corrupted or lost...This apostasy lasted until Heavenly Father and His Beloved Son appeared to Joseph Smith in 1820 and initiated the restoration of the fullness of the gospel...We now live in a time when the gospel of Jesus Christ has been restored.[2]

So, the foundation of Mormonism rests on the claim that all forms of Christianity defected from the truth by the end of the first century. In other words, Christianity died with the apostles. So, Christianity had to be recreated through a new apostle and prophet: enter Joseph Smith.

ORIGINS
Joseph Smith

For over a decade, the manufacturers of *Dos Equis* beer have run a tremendously successful ad campaign using the uber renaissance man motif with their character played by Jonathan Goldsmith. They retired the role in 2019, but his commercials are legendary. Some of the best lines about *the most interesting man in the world* went like this: "His personality is so magnetic that he cannot carry credit cards"; or "He can speak French in Russian"; and "The last time he flirted with danger, danger got clingy." We can only create an ostentatious representation of the most interesting man in the world, whereas, Joseph Smith might actually be the most interesting man in the world.

I know. Discernment ministries, and possibly many others have simply said that Smith was a demon incarnate, or a religious huckster, or a power-hungry occultist. I mean, this is a book entitled *Wolfology*. There is no doubt that Smith is a wolf in sheep's clothing, and there is no denying that he caused many within the sphere of biblical Christianity to stumble. At the same time, objectively speaking, Smith was a spiritual prodigy.

Though he was an opponent of biblical Christianity, one cannot read about this man and not come away thinking that he was remarkable and unique. The late literary critic Harold Bloom called Joseph Smith a "religious genius" who developed a distinctly "American religion."[3] Personally, I think Joseph Smith was a true believer in his ideas, thoughts, and worldview. So, I am not an advocate for the view that Smith started out with a mindset of "trying to take over the world."

Smith was born into a farming family in Sharon, Vermont in 1805. His father, Joseph Smith Sr., had invested his inheritance in a farm that went belly-up by 1816 due to some bad investments. So, the family became tenant farmers to eke out a living. For them, home became Palmyra, New York, the location where Mormonism was born. We cannot forget that western New York during this period of history was still somewhat frontier land, the Wild West so to speak. A spirited revival was taking place throughout New York, Connecticut, and Pennsylvania. Joseph Smith was right in the thick of what would become known as the Second Great Awakening—a time of spiritual excitement and religious fervor. It became routine for Joseph's family to take part in the many revival meetings that came to Palmyra.

Besides, for them, a revival meeting was both a social and spiritual experience. For the Smiths, revival meetings were a part of the routine in the frontier country of western New York. The revivalistic preaching of the day pressed hard for the conversion of souls and demanded the hearers to make a choice to follow Christ. Whitney Cross wrote that practically every time the Smith family went to a revival meeting *"one or another of them would be converted or reconverted each time"* they went. To be fair to the Smith family, my first exposure to fire and brimstone fundamentalism had a similar effect on me. Nevertheless, as much as the Smiths were spiritual, they were equally non-doctrinal.

Joseph's father and mother, Joseph Sr. and Lucy, had little dealings with established churches. Joe Sr. was a product of Unitarianism while Lucy had a mild affiliation with both Methodism and Presbyterianism. The point I want the reader to get is that Smith grew up in a time of great spiritual zeal, removed from the constraints of established orthodoxy, in a home that was deeply spiritual but held a bias against historic Christianity. Dear reader, lean in for these words of warning: *whenever you have spirituality cut off from orthodoxy, heresy will blossom. Always.*

Joseph's Visions

When Joseph Smith was 14 years old, he had a crisis of faith. Given the nature of his cultural context, his parental influences, and his own habits of spirituality, it is not hard to understand why. So, Smith set out to find the purest form of Christianity. Should he become a Baptist, or a Methodist, or a Presbyterian? In 1820, Smith alleges that he was seeking wisdom from the Lord as to which denomination he should join. He went into a nearby forest to pray, but immediately felt oppressed by what he believed to be some diabolical entity. Joseph claimed to be delivered by who he believed to be God the Father and Jesus, the Son. Smith reported,

> I saw two Personages, whose brightness and glory defy all description, standing above me in the air. One of them spake unto me, calling me by name and said, pointing to the other—This is My Beloved Son. Hear Him!

> My object in going to inquire of the Lord was to know which of all the sects was right, that I might know which to join. No sooner, therefore, did I get possession of myself, so as to be able to speak, than I asked the Personages who stood above me in the light,

which of all the sects was right (for at this time it had never entered into my heart that all were wrong)—and which I should join.

I was answered that I must join none of them, for they were all wrong; and the Personage who addressed me said that all their creeds were an abomination in his sight; that those professors were all corrupt.[4]

Over the next 15 years, Smith would allege to having at least 14 visions—including a vision of an angelic host named Moroni, new encounters with Christ, and several apostles (and at least one Old Testament prophet).[5]

The Golden Plates of the Book of Mormon

According to Mormonism, Joseph was chosen by God to restore the church to her early apostolic origins, which meant the sacred writings of *The Book of Mormon* (BOM) needed to be recovered and made available to the world in the final stages of history. These plates had the appearance of gold, and they hung on a D-shaped ring (sort of an ancient heavy-duty *Trapper-Keeper*). Starting in 1823, the angel Moroni visited Smith in a vision and told him that he could find the plates buried in a small stone box upon Hill Cumorah, near Joseph's home.

Moroni had been a prophet-warrior while he was alive, but in his afterlife, he became an angelic host (apparently, you can swap out your humanity and take the form of an angel in the Mormon afterlife). Before his earthly death, Moroni hid the golden plates until such time they needed to be handed to a worthy prophet in the latter-days. Smith was that prophet. He was charged with the task of not only recovering and guarding the plates, but also translating them from Egyptian hieroglyphics into his native English.

The Book of Mormon Story

The BOM and the narrative that it tells is fascinating. It was ahead of its time in terms of "world-building." World building is the process of constructing laws that the writer fixes into the audience's mind; the author should abide by the rules he has created (are you listening Star Wars?). The reading audience expects the writer to have a consistent internal logic that they don't break. The world building of the author(s) of the BOM was an attempt to recreate the biblical world of the ancient Jews and transplant them onto the American continent.

Now you might be wondering, *what is The Book of Mormon really all about?* From my perspective, the BOM is an adventure fantasy tale built with Judeo-Christian language, not to be confused with a fairy tale; likewise, it is both an epic and a tragedy. The BOM begins by telling how the ancient Jaredites fled from Mesopotamia after the Lord confounded the languages of all the people of the earth (Gen 11). According to the BOM, the Jaredites crossed the Atlantic Ocean 2,000 years before the birth of Christ. The second migration happened shortly before the fall of Jerusalem to the Babylonians in 586 B.C.; the BOM reports that Lehi fled Jerusalem with his family and brought a group to the Americas. Eventually, Lehi's tribe became a divided nation made up of the righteous Nephites and the wicked Lamanites.

The Lamanites deserve special attention at this point because according to the BOM, the Lamanites had the color of their skin darkened because of God's curse upon them. Consider how the BOM explains this curse,

> And he had caused the cursing to come upon them, yea, even a sore cursing, because of their iniquity. For behold, they had hardened their hearts against him, that they had become like unto a flint; wherefore, as they were white, and exceedingly fair and delightsome, that they might not be unto my people the Lord God did cause a skin of blackness to come upon them (Nephi 5:21).

The implications of this passage alone have been the cause of much hardship between the LDS and people of color for many years. It is unmistakable; there was a built-in prejudice that the LDS has been trying to correct since the late 1970s when they began to ordain blacks into the priesthood.[6] Nevertheless, this is an important passage because this is the BOM's explanation for the skin color of the Native

American Indians that occupied the lands until the European migrations that occurred in the 15th and 16th centuries.

The most intriguing aspect of the BOM is that it reports that Christ not only spoke to the people audibly as someone speaking on a PA system, but the BOM also reports that Jesus physically appeared to the Nephites after his resurrection. The third book of Nephi is the central narrative of Jesus's appearance to the Nephites; it says:

> And it came to pass, as they understood they cast their eyes up again towards heaven; and behold, they saw a Man descending out of heaven; and he was clothed in a white robe; and he came down and stood in the midst of them, and the eyes of the whole multitude were turned upon him, and they durst not open their mouths, even one to another, and wist [that is, knew] not what it meant, for they thought it was an angel that had appeared unto them. And it came to pass that he stretched forth his hand and spake unto the people, saying: Behold, I am Jesus Christ, whom the prophets testified shall come into the world.[7]

This is an audacious claim, but it is the central claim of the BOM. Reportedly, after Christ ascended once more to heaven (3 Nephi 18:38-39), the Nephites began to have peace with the Lamanites, as the Lamanites were also converted by the message of Jesus.

According to 4 Nephi 1:27, there was peace and prosperity among both the Nephites and the Lamanites, all owing to the appearance of Christ and the spread of his gospel. Churches sprang up everywhere in the land. However, apostasy ended it all with the false churches of the Lamanites persecuting the true churches of the Nephites. In the end, the righteous Nephites perished, save only one—Moroni. Moroni takes the golden plates, named after his father Mormon, and hides them in the stone catacomb in Hill Cumorah in the early 5th century. Ostensibly, these plates are handed over to Joseph Smith in 1823 for translating them into King James English through cleromancy. Cleromancy is a method of determining the divine will of God. A sortition could use several different means to arrive at meaning: rolling of dice, drawing of straws, and even the casting of beans.

The Testimony of the Eleven Witnesses

LDS history says that there were eleven witnesses to the golden plates that Joseph was given to translate.[8] There were initially three: Oliver Cowdery, David Whitmer, and Martin Harris. All of them expressed that the golden plates,

> ...have been translated by the gift and power of God, for his voice hath declared it unto us; wherefore we know of a surety that the work is true. And we also testify that we have seen the engravings which are upon the plates, and they have been shown unto us by the power of God, and not of man.[9]

The testimony of the other eight also corroborated by saying,

> That Joseph Smith, Jun., the translator of this work, has shown unto us the plates of which hath been spoken, which have the appearance of gold; and as many of the leaves as the said Smith has translated we did handle with our hands; and we also saw the engravings thereon, all of which has the appearance of an ancient work.[10]

Several books have been written on the validity of the testimony of the eleven men. Some approach the evidence of these men by attacking their character—implying that they are liars. Others approach the testimony of these men by pointing out that some of them had close family ties—meaning that they are biased and co-conspirators.

Although I think there is some validity to questioning the credibility of the witnesses, I also think that attacking the character of the witnesses is an ineffective way of debunking the myth of the golden plates. At times, apologetic websites get into arguments about how impractical it would be to use heavy golden plates, due to their dense weight; they tend to get into long, tedious discussions about metals and dimensions. However, I think that history has given us a better answer.

Emma Smith, Joseph's first wife, explained in an 1879 interview that Joseph translated the BOM by way of esoteric means; basically, Emma attested that Joseph never referred to golden plates or any other manuscript. Instead, he used a peep stone and a hat and dictated what he saw in his trance (Emma never saw the plates either, only something that was alleged to be the plates covered in cloth).[11]

Joseph was no stranger to divining. His history of practicing necromancy is notorious.[12] The magical elements of Joseph's life is a fact that even Mormon historians concede, although they treat it as the mere "foibles" of a teenage boy.[13] It is quite possible that those witnesses who alleged to have seen the golden plates of the BOM only saw them in a spiritually-ecstatic way. Or their minds were so pliable they saw what they wanted to see, or more deviously—they saw what Joseph wanted them to see. It is not out of the question. Even in hypercharismatic contexts of today, there are some who allege seeing gold dust or angel's feathers fall from the rafters on a rowdy-holy-rolling Sunday morning.[14]

MORMONISM'S EVOLUTION
Always Changing

Joseph Smith is the architect of the Mormon religion; nobody doubts that. He remains integral to the foundations of the LDS church because everything hangs on Prophet Smith's testimony. Mormons are not gamblers (at least they are not supposed to be), but they are certainly wagering that Smith's visions of Jesus are true. That is not to say that Mormonism has not evolved from its inception in 1830. Mormonism started in New York, then moved to Ohio, then down to Missouri, and over to Illinois—finally settling in Salt Lake City, Utah. Mormonism has gone through geographical changes as well as changes in doctrine. The one constant with Mormonism is that it remains in flux.

Purportedly, the LDS church has always received fresh revelation from God throughout its short history. In many ways, Mormonism was built like the applications we use for our smartphones; it was never meant to be inert. Instead, it is constantly being updated. For example, Joseph Smith and the early patriarchs of the Mormon religion practiced polygamy as a spiritual principle until the U.S. government threatened federal intervention in the late 19th century. Then suddenly, Mormon President Wilford Woodruff caught a dose of the Holy Ghost and a manifesto went out, and the practice ended; at least among the popularized version of the LDS movement that we know today (some radical movements that branched out from the LDS illegally practice it). Similarly, in 1978 the LDS church changed its views on race and some of the prohibitions against persons of color and began to ordain blacks into the office of the priesthood.

Mormonism is sort of like a chameleon (and I don't mean that in a pejorative sense). It knows how to adapt to its surrounding and makes the proper adjustments to survive and thrive. Though Joseph Smith said, "The Book of Mormon was the most correct of any book on earth, and the keystone of our religion and a man would get nearer to God by abiding by its precepts, than by any other book,"[15] the current BOM has undergone updated iterations as well as thousands of alterations.[16]

However, if you believe that a living prophet gives modern revelation from God and routinely updates the framework of your religious belief system, then anything is possible. This is part of the uniqueness of Mormonism. It was built to advance, grow, and develop. Evangelical Christians who come from a creedal and confessional background stand diametrically opposed to this way of thinking (and you can count me among them).

Conversely, Smith held a strong animus towards creeds and confessions, not wanting a religion tied to what he believed to be stone-cold orthodoxy. Instead, Smith preached about a deity who spoke and revealed himself through dreams and visions, who sent angelic messengers, and was restoring the church of Jesus in these latter days to a living prophet. Thus, a religion that does not have a static set of doctrines can do just about anything it wants.

Mormonism Right Now

The LDS is characterized by a short history with peaks and valleys. In its earlier days, there was no shortage of violence that surrounded it. For instance, Joseph Smith was shot to death by vigilantes in Nauvoo, Illinois, in 1843. Likewise, in 1857, a group of militant Mormons known as the "Nauvoo Legion" murdered over 100 settlers in what has become known as *the Mountain Meadow Massacre*. However, Mormonism has grown into what many consider a civilized and well-organized reconstruction of Christianity. Mormons have four canonical books that inform their faith: *The Bible*, insofar as it is interpreted correctly; *The Book of Mormon*; *The Doctrines and Covenants*; and *The Pearl of Great Price*. But ultimately, the source of authority in the LDS is centered upon their living prophet (more commonly known as the President). The current LDS President as of this writing, Russell N. Nelson, was ordained to lead the church following the death of Thomas Monson, in 2018.

Since its beginnings, Mormonism has grown exponentially over the last 190 years. Starting with less than 80 members, Mormonism now boasts of 16.5 million members worldwide, with close to 7 million living in the United States.[17] They have missionary efforts that in some ways put Protestant Evangelicals to shame. The LDS church statistics report that there are close to 67,000 active Mormon missionaries.[18] By comparison, Mormons have seven times as many missionaries serving than the Southern Baptist Convention (the largest Protestant denomination in the United States).

The LDS church has gone from an isolated group that was off the grid to becoming mainstream and active in all spheres of society. Brigham Young University, named after Joseph Smith's successor, has a tremendous reputation for first-rate academics, as well as several notable alums: former GOP presidential nominee Mitt Romney; author and entrepreneur Stephen Covey; and novelist Orson Scott Card. The LDS is also known for its incredible generosity and charity.

Mormonism began small and has evolved into a larger entity marked by faith and action; and although the heart of what they believe about God and Christ is strange to Evangelicals, many of them remain sincere in their beliefs. My own personal interaction with Mormons has been overwhelmingly positive. Mormon scholars that I have reached out to in order to discuss aspects of my research have been incredibly helpful, as I have tried to dig deep into the history of Joseph Smith and the Mormon religion. The culture that the LDS church has created is commendable. However, a closer look shows that the theology of Mormonism is incompatible with historic Christianity.

STRANGER THINGS: LDS DOCTRINES
Restoring Christianity

Joseph Smith alleges that God revealed to him the need for apostolic Christianity to be restored because it had fallen into apostasy. Mormonism is an attempt to criticize the anti-supernaturalism and the ultra-rationalism that Smith observed in the Protestant churches of his own day and time. In some ways, his criticism is as just now, as it was back then. However, by Smith's own doctrines, he explicitly rejects the apostolic faith that he claims to restore.

Godhead

Mormons reject the trinitarian nature of the Christian Godhead. Instead, Mormonism opts for a tritheistic-polytheism. Let us break that down a little bit. Tritheism is a belief in three separate gods, which implies polytheism (many gods), thus, denying the monotheistic nature of Judeo-Christianity (Dt 6:4-9). Smith is blunt about his perspectives; he once said:

> I will preach on the plurality of Gods. I have selected this text for that express purpose. I wish to declare I have always and in all congregations when I have preached on the subject of the Deity, it has been the plurality of Gods...I have always declared God to be a distinct personage, Jesus Christ a separate and distinct personage from God the Father, and that the Holy Ghost was a distinct personage and a Spirit...We have three Gods anyhow, and they are plural: and who can contradict it?[19]

Polytheism is also inherent in the eschatology of Mormonism because they believe in the teaching called *the exaltation of man*. The exaltation of man means that only good and faithful Mormons who follow the *articles of faith* and *the words of wisdom*, give faithfully to the LDS church, serve on the mission field, and are sealed with temple rites can be elevated from humanity to deity.

Of course, the exaltation of man is not only about humanity's divine potential, but it also implies that the god of "our" universe was once a man too. There is a popular couplet that was coined back in 1840 by Lorenzo Snow (5th President of the LDS church), it goes like this: "as man now is, God once was; as God is, man may *become.*"[20] There has been some contemporary debate about the relevance of this teaching within the LDS church in the last twenty years. There are some who believe that Mormonism may be taking the proper steps to conform to a set of doctrines that is more in line with the historic Christian faith.[21] However, that remains to be seen. For all the wild stories that surround Mormonism, one thing is brutishly clear—the LDS understanding of the Godhead rejects historic Christianity.

Jesus

As mentioned above, in the LDS faith, Jesus is a distinct and separate being from God the Father. This is a rejection of Nicene Christianity. Historic Christianity has argued for 1700 years that Christ is of the same substance of God the Father, but in the Mormon model, Jesus is only a man with the potential to become a god. Likewise, Mormonism also falls into the Arian trap. If God the Father had a beginning and was once a man like us, it would mean that Jesus is not eternal, either. In which case, Mormonism could add Arius' *Thalia* to the official LDS songbook, singing "there was a time when he was not."

Salvation

In Mormonism, everyone gets saved to a degree. What I mean is that Mormonism defaults to a form of Universalism in their views of the hereafter. According to LDS teaching, there are *three Kingdoms of Glory* in the afterlife. The first is *the Celestial Kingdom*. It is the grand prize. Only good Mormons who have served faithfully and have gone to the temple can graduate to "the exaltation of man" that we explored earlier.

Second is *the Terrestrial Kingdom.* The Terrestrial Kingdom is reserved for bad Mormons (those who embraced Joseph Smith but did not perform good works) and good Christians (the ones who did not embrace Joseph Smith and the fullness of the Gospel), it is not quite Heaven, but more like an eternity on a beach in the Bahamas with cold drinks and the little umbrellas that go in them.

Last is *the Telestial Kingdom,* a place for pagans, hypocritical Christians and hypocritical Mormons—it is not Heaven, and it is not eternity at the beach either—it is probably more like living in Siberia during the winter, much closer to a Roman Catholic view of purgatory. As well, Mormons do have a place reserved for the sons of *perdition*. When I was growing up, it was called *Outer Darkness* (remember, within the LDS things change). Perdition is reserved for the vilest, most sinister of people who denied God and rejected His truth; or for Mormon apostates who have left the LDS church.

It is worth mentioning that salvation can also be obtained after a person dies. This is where the Mormon's teaching of *baptisms for the dead* comes into play, but we are not going down that rabbit hole. Instead, it is enough for the reader to understand that the LDS has a high view of post-mortem salvation. They believe it would be unfair of God to not allow every person who lived on earth a chance to hear the Gospel and respond. So, for all non-Mormons, they get a chance to hear the gospel and choose to receive Christ or reject him.

Now you might be wondering, *where does Jesus fit into the salvation of souls?* According to the LDS articles of faith, Jesus remains a central figure in the redemption of humanity. The third and fourth articles of the LDS faith state:

We believe that through the Atonement of Christ, all man-kind may be saved, by obedience to the laws and ordinances of the Gospel. We believe that the first principles and ordinances of the Gospel are: first, Faith in the Lord Jesus Christ; second, Repentance; third, Baptism by immersion for the remission of sins; fourth, Laying on of hands for the gift of the Holy Ghost.[22]

If you just glance at these two articles, you might come away thinking that they sound just like anything you would hear in a Christian worship service. But keep a close eye on the following statement that *Ensign* (the LDS flagship publication) made in 2005, "If your friends ask, 'Does your church believe you are saved by grace or works?' you could say, 'We believe that we are saved by grace *after all we can do*. We don't earn salvation. Heavenly Father and the Savior will bless us with eternal life, through Their grace, *if we do our part*.'"[23] In other words, if you asked a Mormon if they are saved by grace through faith in Jesus, they could say "yes." However, they would reinforce it quickly by saying, "But you must do what is required of you, or else."

This is one of the reasons why LDS teaching is so harmful. The language they use and the way that it gets applied is slippery. I am not questioning their intent. I have always believed Mormons to be sincere in what they believe. Nonetheless, there is an internal inconsistency within Mormonism, almost an uneasiness about being saved by God's free grace. For instance, if you were to open a Bible with a set of LDS missionaries and started to read Ephesians 2:4-9, emphasizing that we are "saved by grace through faith" to them, they would approve it in every way. But in a blink-of-an-eye, they would likely turn to James 2:17 and say, "faith without works is dead."

This further confirms their uneasiness about a biblical understanding of salvation by grace alone. Evangelical Protestants understand that we are as the saying goes, *saved by faith alone, but that faith is never alone*. But Mormons cannot get around it; no matter how much they equivocate, because in the end, they affirm on one hand that they are saved by grace and on the other hand works. Whereas Christians believe that we are saved by grace (Rom 3:19-26; 11:6) and in turn, we do good works (Eph 2:10); Mormons believe that they are saved by grace and their good works. This teaching is not the Gospel of Christ.

Same Language, Different Meaning

The issue of language has been pointed out well by Christian theologians and apologists for some time now. An unsuspecting person who knows church-lingo could easily fall into the thinking that Mormon missionaries are speaking the same language as Baptists, Methodists, or Presbyterians. For example, if we talk about salvation by faith in Jesus, a Mormon missionary might say, "We believe we are saved by faith in Jesus too." As an example, let us define who Jesus is in accordance with both Mormon and Christian teaching.

For Mormons, they believe that Jesus's nature is of a different substance than of God the Father, that there was a time in eternity when Jesus did not exist, and that Jesus is another god among many gods. But for Christians who affirm the apostolic faith, we affirm that Jesus is the second person of the Holy Trinity (Mt 28:19), that Jesus is the eternal Son of God who has no beginning and no end (Jn 1:1-2), that Jesus is one with the Father with distinction, but without separation (Heb 1:3). This is just one example among many.

LESSONS IN WOLFOLOGY

1. A SUPERFICIAL CHRISTIAN DOES NOT STAND A CHANCE AGAINST A MORMON WITH CONVICTIONS.

Mormons affirm things that fly in the face of biblical Christianity: a rejection of monotheism, that humanity can become divine, that Jesus came to the Americas and cursed the Lamanites with more melanin in their skin. Mormonism is strange, but it has nonetheless grown into a religious powerhouse. Why?

In the early 1980s, the LDS mission's movement drew ex-Southern Baptists into Mormon fellowships at alarming rates.[24] *How could something like that happen?* It happens when you have doctrinal commitments that have all the tensile strength of a stale graham cracker. I do not think nominal Christians with loose doctrinal roots could stand toe-to-

toe with a Mormon who has deep convictions about their faith. Without a robust theological anchor, it is easy for some to get swept away by deceit (Eph 4:14). The way forward for Evangelicals is to thicken our orthodoxy, be consistent in the discipleship of believers with the Word of God, and the church needs her pastors and elders to be faithful watchmen who protect the sheep and send the wolves to flight.

2. DON'T GO DOWN THE MORMON RABBIT HOLE.

Where I am from, people use the expression "don't go down the rabbit hole." It is what happens when you get caught in some of the complex, confusing, and bizarre natures of a given subject. Mormonism fits that description well. I remember trying to teach about Mormonism to a Sunday School class many years ago. The teenagers were interested in the topic (I thought, "wow, miracles still happen"). But as I started fielding questions about Mormonism's views of the afterlife, I got questions coming in from all directions.

One of them asked me a question about how Jesus came to the American continent. Then I got asked a question about the angel Moroni. Then someone asked about the practice of polygamy. This went on for a good twenty minutes, and then all the sudden everyone soon lost interest. Why? Because it was too puzzling to follow. The best thing I could do was state the simple facts of the case and show the primary areas of Mormonism that are incompatible with Christianity, emphasizing three areas: first, the differences between a Christian understanding of the Trinity and Mormonism's tritheism; second, the Christian understanding of monotheism while pointing out Mormonism's polytheism; and finally, contrasting the Christian and Mormon concepts of salvation.

3. MORMONISM IS FURTHER AFFIRMATION THAT THE CHRISTIAN GOSPEL WILL ALWAYS HAVE FALSE GOSPELS WITH WHICH TO COMPETE.

Paul said in Galatians 1:6-7 "I am astonished that you are so quickly deserting him who called you in the grace of Christ and are turning to a different gospel—not that there is another one, but there are some who trouble you and want to distort the gospel of Christ." There have been counterfeit gospels since the days of the apostles. Mormonism presents a counterfeit gospel in one of the most explicit ways imaginable. Just consider the front cover of the BOM for a moment. It literally says *The Book of Mormon: ANOTHER TESTAMENT OF JESUS CHRIST.* Talk about stating the obvious. Mormonism is intentionally competing with the Christian gospel.

Christianity is surrounded by competing gospels (some are mentioned in this book), like the prosperity gospel, the moral-therapeutic gospel, the Christless man-centered gospel. The danger to the church, nominals, and non-Christians is that there is a dark allure about false gospels that seduces our hearts. Trevin Wax gives a warning about imitation gospels, stating,

> A counterfeit gospel will always leave our souls impoverished at just the point we should be enriched … Counterfeits are like candy. They may be pleasant to the taste, but they leave us spiritualty malnourished.[25]

4. GET GOOD AT DEFINING YOUR TERMS.

My pastor and mentor, Charlie Shields, constantly told me to do the following: *always define your terminology.* This is especially true when interacting with Mormons (honestly, it is a good principle for most situations). Never be afraid to ask a Mormon missionary or a Mormon neighbor during a time of friendly dialogue: *What do you mean by salvation by grace? Or what do you mean that you believe the Bible so long as it is interpreted correctly?* This is especially important as you deal with the nature of the Godhead and the person of Christ.

5. JESUS'S NAME AND JESUS'S NATURE: THE TWO ARE NOT ALWAYS THE SAME.

Building off the previous point about defining your terms, our LDS friends think that they believe in the same Jesus that you believe in. They reason this way, "The Jesus of the Bible is the same Jesus of *The Book of Mormon.*" However, this is where we need to make a distinction between the *name of Jesus and the nature of Jesus.* Just because

Mormons believe in a savior by the name of Jesus and locate him in the Bible and the BOM does not mean he is the true Jesus of the Bible. This is where we have to shed light on the nature of Jesus so that our Mormon friends might see.

We must emphasize that Jesus is not a man who became a god. Jesus is God who became a man (Jn 1:1-14). Jesus did not become a god but is forever the God-man (Rev 1:8; 2:23). Jesus is not separate from the Father but is distinct from the Father, yet, without separation (Jn 10:30; 17:20; Mt 11:27). Jesus is not less than God but is equal to God (Heb 1:3-4). Jesus did not come into existence as a creature of God's creation; instead, Jesus has always been co-eternal with God the Father and God the Spirit in perfect Trinity (Jn 1:1-2, 17:5).

Multiple times in the New Testament, Christians are warned about people who would try to do a Jesus cosplay and pawn themselves off as the Son of God. Paul warns about this in 2nd Corinthians 11:4. Jesus teaches about it in the context of the final days of history in Matthew 24:24, stating, "For false christs and false prophets will arise and perform great signs and wonders, so as to lead astray, if possible, even the elect." Scripture warns us that there are a lot of false prophets who will come claiming to be Jesus. Doctrinally discerning Christians will know Jesus not only by His name but also by His nature.

Joseph Smith's Mormonism has blossomed into more than he could have ever imagined. There are even aspects of Mormonism that Evangelical Christians can respect, such as their charitable contributions to the impoverished. But when you get right down to it, Mormonism presents false gods, a false christ, and a false gospel. The LDS began with a desire to restore Christianity to her apostolic origins, but the facts do not bear that out. If you trade the Jesus of the Bible for the Jesus of Mormonism—or if you exchange the Gospel of Christ for the Gospel of Joseph Smith, or if you substitute the historic Christian doctrine of the triune God with the LDS doctrine of tritheism—you have not restored Christianity, you have lost Christianity.

But concerning that day and hour no one knows, not even the angels of heaven, nor the Son, but the Father only. For as were the days of Noah, so will be the coming of the Son of Man.

—Jesus of Nazareth, Matthew 24:36-37

Jehovah's Witnesses

Mark Twain wrote, "Man is the religious animal. He is the only religious animal. He is the only animal that has the True Religion—several of them."[1] Twain's sentiments are not only humorous but accurate. Some things are never in flux: the sun rises in the east and sets in the west, what goes up must come down, and man will always worship someone or something. If a man cannot find a religion that suits him, he will have no problem inventing one that will.

It reminds me of the 1986 movie *Highlander*. My wife Rachel was a big *Highlander* nerd when it was spun-off into a TV show during the 1990s. It was her everyday midday vice: PB&J, chips and dip, and an immortal Scot warrior wielding a sword trying to hack off the heads of his enemies. Ah, the good ol' days. The premise of the show is straightforward—the Immortals must seek, hunt, and destroy the other remaining Immortals in a duel to decide who will win "the prize." The motto of the show was, "There can be only one." The show chronicled an elimination tournament that spanned thousands of years across the globe. Similarly, Christianity has competed with other religious movements that make exclusive claims to be the sole gatekeepers of salvation.

Those who follow Islamic teachings are told in the Quran that "whoever defies the Messenger after guidance has become clear to them and follows a path other than that of the believers, We will let them pursue what they have chosen, then burn them in Hell."[2] The Church of Jesus Christ of Latter-day Saints (Chapter 4), has taught since its inception that they are "the one and only true living church on the face of the earth."[3] The Jehovah's Witnesses have made similar exclusivist claims.

Consider a couple of examples from *The Watchtower Society*, which expressed that "Jehovah is using *only one* organization today to accomplish his will. To receive everlasting life in the earthly Paradise we must identify that organization and serve God as part of it."[4] In the 1990 book, *You Can Live Forever,* it states that, "You must be part of Jehovah's organization, doing God's will, in order to receive his blessing of everlasting life."[5]

A further example comes from a mid-20th century tract that simply explains, "One who professes to be a Christian must always be part of Jehovah's visible organization."[6] These are not isolated instances; instead, they are at the heart of the Jehovah's Witnesses organization. On the Jehovah's Witnesses' website (jw.org) it states quite clearly that, "Jesus Christ didn't agree with the view that there are many religions, many roads, all leading to salvation…Jehovah's Witnesses believe that they've found that road. Otherwise, they'd look for another religion."[7]

ORIGINS
Charles Taze Russell

Remember Arianism (Chapter 1)? Well, Arianism is alive and well today. It is preserved in the Jehovah's Witnesses. The organization started in 1870 as an offshoot from the William Miller-led Adventist movement when Charles Taze Russell (1852-1916) began an independent Bible study that was primarily focused on the second coming of Christ.[8] Russell would be the figurehead for the movement for almost half a century. Born in Allegheny, Pennsylvania, on February 16, 1852, Russell was raised in the Presbyterian tradition.[9] By his teenage years,

Russell had grown tired of the creedalism of his religious tradition as well as the doctrines concerning eternal punishment.[10]

Around 1870, Russell fell in with the Adventists and became enamored by their zeal for the imminent return of Jesus Christ. By 1875, Russell had fallen out of company with the Adventists and sought to proclaim his own understanding of prophecy, and how it opened a window into eschatological forecasting. The popularity of his brand of Bible teaching caught on.

By the summer of 1879, Russell had developed a monthly magazine to proliferate his teachings to the masses. Initially called *Zion's Watchtower and Herald of Christ's Presence*, the magazine would become known as *The Watchtower*, a monthly repository of Jehovah's Witnesses' teaching. The publishing efforts of *The Watch Tower Bible and Tract Society* served as one of the primary proselytizing tools and ensured the steady growth of Russell's new movement.[11] Additionally, Russell's many books helped bring his ideas to the masses, books like *The Divine Plan for the Ages* (1886), or *Studies in Scripture* (1886), and *The Time is at Hand* (1904).

Russell took his views of the apocalypse to epic proportions by explaining that Christ had returned to the world invisibly in 1874; a prediction Russell called "the harvest" in 1878—the view that God's faithful would be transformed spiritually.[12] When Jesus did not return, like many end-of-time speculators, Russell just gave another prediction, this time 1881 (I can hear the slogan now: "Now's the time for fun, Christ returns in eighty-one). Of course, when the 1881 return did not happen, Russell further predicted future dates that went unfulfilled. One might think predictive failures would have been the end of the road for Russell, but in fact, the movement grew to 50,000 adherents by 1914 (I guess failing upwards not only applies to politicians but also false teachers).[13]

Russell courted controversy, not only over failed predictions but also his failed marriage. In 1897, his wife of 18 years—Maria Frances Ackley—filed for divorce over allegations that Russell had molested their foster daughter, Rose Ball.[14] Russell rejected Ackley's testimony as mere spite, the accusations of a woman towards her husband with whom she had no small amount of animosity. However, the court did rule in Ackley's favor, and she was awarded alimony. Russell refused to pay; instead, he gave his assets to the Watchtower Society as a way of circumventing the court's judgment.[15] It does not appear that Ball ever made any public comments on the truthfulness of the allegations of sexual abuse.

Joseph Rutherford

When Russell passed away in 1916, Joseph Rutherford (1869-1942) carried the Jehovah's Witnesses forward to the middle of the 20th century. As M. James Penton points out, "Rutherford was a very different man from Russell," explaining,

> Instead of growing up in a big-city atmosphere under the loving guidance of a prosperous and benevolent father, Rutherford had to work very hard in near poverty. By dint of great personal effort, he studied law under the old apprentice system then quite common in the United States and passed his bar examinations in 1892...he developed a strong personality, an outspoken although seldom-manifested sympathy for the downtrodden, and a thoroughgoing contempt for big business, politicians, and later, the clergy.[16]

Rutherford's story is the all-American one that people in the United States extol—through grit and self-determination, Rutherford made himself into a formidable man in challenging times.

However, there are aspects of Rutherford's life that can remind some of us of that old-crank, Archie Bunker; at times a foul-mouth, at other times a raging alcoholic.[17] Nevertheless, Rutherford would not be a poor substitute for Russell. As Brigham Young was to Joseph Smith in his succession, so too was Rutherford to Russell in his. However, some heads would have to roll first. In 1917, Rutherford seized control of the Watch Tower Society with a hostile takeover of the organization, removing four members of the board of directors and replacing them with his loyalists.[18] In 1931, Rutherford would re-brand the movement as the *Jehovah's Witnesses*.[19] Although often considered a rough-edge, Rutherford's tactics carried the Jehovah's Witnesses to new heights.

How were those heights reached? Most likely, through autocratic control that Rutherford exercised over his expanding organization.[20] Rutherford's cunning and occasional ruthlessness brought about the seeds for his theocratic vision for the Watch Tower Society.[21] Regardless of what one might think of Rutherford's schemes, the organization's successes were stunning. Another factor was Rutherford's massive post-WWI campaign based on a book by the same name called *Millions Now Living Will Never Die*.[22] Although dynamic and controversial, Rutherford continued to advance the apocalyptic fervor that captivated so many that by the time of his death the Jehovah's Witnesses numbered 127,478.[23]

Global Rise of the Jehovah's Witnesses

Nathan Homer Knorr (1905-1977) was elected to replace Rutherford in January 1942.[24] A native of Bethlehem, Pennsylvania, Knorr's disposition was milder than Rutherford's by a country mile. Yet Knorr was no less committed to the common cause of the global expansion of the Watch Tower Society. Knorr was a calculating businessman who lacked the dynamism of both Russell and Rutherford. Likewise, he lacked the literary chops of his predecessors; that is why early in his tenure he instituted that all Watch Tower Society material be published anonymously.

Given Knorr's theological deficits and subpar writing abilities, ironically, Knorr's crowning achievement was the publishing of the *New World Translation* (NWT) *of the Holy Scriptures*. Produced in 1950, the NWT had a distinctly Jehovah's Witnesses' perspective, mainly because it adds the indefinite article in John 1:1, which reads, "In the beginning was the Word, and the Word was with God, *and the Word was a god.*"[25]

Though Knorr was known for lacking charisma, he made up for it with his zeal for the movement's expansion. Out of the first three presidents of the Watch Tower Society, Knorr may be the most capable leader the sect has ever known. Knorr's proselytizing efforts exceeded all others before him. By 1970 the Jehovah's Witnesses exceeded 1 million *Publishers,* practically multiplying the movement ten-fold in three short decades.[26] Today, according to the Jehovah's Witnesses' official website, they have 8.7 million adherents in 240 countries worldwide.[27] Some reports even tout the Jehovah's Witnesses as one of the fastest-growing religions in North America.[28]

THEOLOGICAL BELIEFS
Jehovah's Witnesses' Understanding of God

The Jehovah's Witnesses, in line with classic Arianism, reject the Triune nature of God—contending that "The Father is God alone."[29] In official writings, the Jehovah's Witnesses are forthright in their convictions, stating "The dogma of the Trinity is not found in the Bible, nor is it in harmony with what the Bible teaches. It grossly misrepresents the true God."[30] Furthermore, as Lucas Butler explains,

> [to a member of the Jehovah's Witnesses] If a particular doctrine cannot be reasonably explained, it is likely unsound. Witnesses reject the doctrine of the Trinity for this reason, among others. The mystery of God in three persons defies human reason; therefore, it cannot be a sound doctrine.[31]

Additionally, the Jehovah's Witnesses focus on the name "Jehovah" as the exclusive name to be used for God. Often, they cite Isaiah 43:10, "'You are my witnesses,' declares the LORD, 'and my servant whom I have chosen.'" Practically speaking, by emphasizing that Jehovah is the one and only name to be used for God, they intentionally reject the deity of both Christ and the Holy Spirit.

Jehovah's Witnesses' Understanding of Jesus

Where does Jesus fit into the Jehovah's Witnesses' realm of ideas? Helpful here is Bruce Metzger's analysis, as he explains:

One of the continuing features of this sect is that it remains a modern form of the ancient heresy of Arianism. According to the Jehovah's Witnesses, Christ before his earthly life was a spirit-creature named Michael, the first of God's creation, through whom God made the other created things. As a consequence of his birth on earth, which was not an incarnation, Jesus became a perfect human being, the equal of Adam prior to the Fall. In his death, Jesus' human nature, being sacrificed, was annihilated. As a reward for his sacrificial obedience, God gave him a divine, spirit nature. Throughout his existence, therefore, Jesus Christ never was co-equal with God. He is not eternal, for there was a time when he was not. While he was on earth he was nothing more than a man, and therefore the atoning effect of his death can have no more significance than that of a perfect human being.[32]

In this theological framework, Jesus is much less than God but is much more than man. Just when we thought Arianism was dead, it has found a thriving home in Kingdom Halls all over the world.

Jehovah's Witnesses' Understanding of the Holy Spirit

According to their website, the Jehovah's Witnesses confess that "The holy spirit is God's power in action, his active force. God sends out his spirit by projecting his energy to any place to accomplish his will."[33] In this conception, the Holy Spirit is reduced to an impersonal cosmic force, an instrument of power. This view eliminates any notion of the Holy Spirit as a divine person who exists eternally and equally with the Father.

In one fell swoop, the Jehovah's Witnesses terminate the Trinity, reject the humanity and deity of Jesus, and reduce the Spirit of God to an impersonal ray of divine power. The Jehovah's Witnesses reject these doctrines with the often-heard appeal of restorationists, "No creed but the Bible." Because the word Trinity is notably absent from the Bible, with extreme inflexibility, they say the notion of Trinity must be a man-made invention. The late R.C. Sproul handled this objection quite capably when he wrote:

All that the word Trinity does is capture the scriptural teaching linguistically on the unity of God and the tri-personality of God. Seeing these concepts in Scripture, we search for a word that accurately communicates them...It really is naive to object that the word itself is not found in Scripture if the concept is found in Scripture and is taught by Scripture.[34]

As unconventional as it may sound, sometimes we must use non-biblical language to convey a biblical concept. Besides, the doctrine of Trinity cannot be reduced to a singular text. Instead, the whole counsel of God's Word reveals it from creation to redemption and to consummation.

Salvation in the Jehovah's Witnesses

As a religious movement, no one can deny that the Jehovah's Witnesses continues to grow. Much of this growth is "conversion" growth, which is owing to the incredible outreach efforts of the movement.[35] I have been solicited by many sincere followers of the Jehovah's Witnesses throughout my life. From cruise terminals throughout the Bahamas to the canal walk in Indianapolis, you can find Jehovah's Witnesses' kiosks in practically every corner of the globe. I imagine it makes Southern Baptist church growth strategists a little jealous to some degree. It drives you to ask: *why are so many attracted to this movement?*

The question recalls a time my friend, Chuck, told me that when he was getting married and settling down that he wanted to lay down some religious foundations for his family (he was raised in a non-Christian home). Chuck was a disciplined man but had some rough edges that still needed to be smoothed out. As he surveyed the landscape of religious options, he was at first drawn to Roman Catholicism. He reasoned (and I mean no offense, but these were his words), "If I become Catholic I can still drink and gamble." That is an overly reductionistic view of Roman Catholicism, at the same time the point Chuck was making was that from his perspective Roman Catholicism was *easy.*

However, if you ask anyone who has been associated with the Jehovah's Witnesses for any length of time, they will tell you that it is far from easy. Salvation in the context of the Jehovah's Witnesses surfs on the wave of strict obedience.

The Jehovah's Witnesses' website (jw.org) is full of resources that consistently teach the same message, "To gain salvation, you must exercise faith in Jesus and demonstrate that faith by obeying his commands. The Bible shows that you must have works, or acts of obedience, to prove that your faith is alive."[36] The language is strikingly similar to that of Evangelical Christianity. However, there are countless records of people who have left the Jehovah's Witnesses that reported that salvation was a merit system of sorts; for example, those who are saved are those who are zealous in their outreach efforts, adhere to a strict moral code, and abstain from the secular world. The Jehovah's Witnesses do not deny the need for God's grace, nor do they deny the need for repentance and faith. However, the accent for salvation tends to fall not on grace, but obedience.

Another puzzling part of the Jehovah's Witnesses' understanding of salvation is where the atoning work of Christ fits into the picture. The Jehovah's Witnesses have two key concepts related to their knowledge of Christ's atonement: 1) Jesus was born as a perfect man, like Adam, but remained perfectly obedient where Adam failed; 2) By Jesus's perfect obedience he "cancelled out the effect of Adam's disobedience."[37] The Jehovah's Witnesses use the language of "corresponding ransom." The basic premise is that Jesus had to pay with his life what Adam lost with his disobedience.[38]

At first glance, it seems like the Jehovah's Witnesses share a similar understanding of the atonement with Evangelicals, however, remember that according to the Jehovah's Witnesses, Jesus is the pre-incarnate Archangel Michael, and then born as a perfect man. The Jehovah's Witnesses make no attempts to resolve this incredible dilemma—*is Jesus an angel, or is he a man?* The Jehovah's Witnesses simply answer: Jesus was an angel in the preexistence, then Jesus became a man while on earth, and then Jesus became "a spirit creature" in his resurrection.[39] Furthermore, if Jesus became a perfect man, it just reinforces the Jehovah's Witnesses' denial of Christ's miraculous incarnation of God in human flesh. Moreover, Jehovah's Witnesses believe that Jesus's resurrection was not a physical one, but a spiritual one only. The Jehovah's Witnesses officially believe that Jesus "...would not be resurrected with his flesh-and-blood body."[40]

ESCHATOLOGY
Heaven and Earth: Two Tiers of Salvation

As mentioned above, there is a heavy emphasis within the Watch Tower Society's legalist approach to salvation. A works-based salvation is consistent with the two-tiered approach to eternal rewards that are built into the Jehovah's Witnesses' frame of thought; some may even consider it a caste system of sorts. For instance, the Jehovah's Witnesses believe that "heavenly" salvation is restricted to a small group (compared to all the people who are alive now or will ever live) of individuals (the Anointed), while there will be another group (the Great Crowd) that will enjoy life on earth forever.[41] So, salvation is not equally applied—some get the penthouse—while others get the outhouse.

Now lest the reader think that I am sensationalizing Jehovah's Witnesses' exclusivism, just read the words from a Jehovah's Witness manual of beliefs that explains, "Salvation is open to just as many people as will demonstrate true faith in the provision that God has made through Jesus, but the Bible says that only 144,000 will go to heaven to be with Christ."[42] Once more, this speaks to the faulty hermeneutics of the Jehovah's Witnesses and an interpretive approach that seems reluctant to harmonize the 144,000 of Revelation 7 with the parts of Scripture that emphasize that "many" will be saved (Mt 8:11; 20:28; Rom 5:15, 19-20).

Hell

Charles Taze Russell always kicked against the doctrine of eternal torment—his acrimony towards the wrath of God has been well documented. Russell's hatred of divine punishment has shaped the Jehovah's Witnesses organization since its inception. Butler explains:

> Concerning the eternal torment in hell, the Witnesses believe that this doctrine is another one of Satan's lies…The devil attempts to convince the world that God tortures people for eternity. Jehovah is a God of love and he would never make anyone suffer in such an extreme fashion.[43]

So, what happens to the wicked? They are simply annihilated.[44] Like a Thanos snap—they are ash-flakes in the blowing wind.

CONTROVERSY
Failed Predictions Concerning the Second Coming of Jesus Christ

As mentioned before, the foundations for the Jehovah's Witnesses really began over predictions about the return of Christ. In that the Jehovah's Witnesses are an offshoot of William Miller's Adventist movement, it is unsurprising that it held similar convictions about the imminent return of Christ. Russell soon made his own predictions on the "basis of the book of Daniel," as well his belief that "the Great Pyramid of Gizeh" held some of the clues that one would need to calculate the return of Christ.[45]

Russell taught early on that Jesus had returned in October of 1874, at least spiritually speaking. This has caused no small amount of embarrassment because Russell also predicted that Christ would return in 1914. However, when the Lord stayed at the right hand of God and did not come at the Watch Tower's beckoning, the organization had to pull out the old "Jesus returned invisibly" line again.[46] The Watch Tower Society held firm to the idea that Jesus was overthrowing "human governments."[47] Despite the embarrassment, the Jehovah's Witnesses pressed on and continued to gain a following.

Then came the teaching that "Abraham would be alive in 1925." Actually, several Old Testament saints were promised to return in 1925, men like Abraham, Isaac, Jacob, and the Prophets were to return to the earth as a grandiose witness for Jehovah.[48] I have this nightmarish thought of Hosea learning how to do the Charleston (oh, the horrors of a sinful imagination). Anyway, 1925 came and went with no miracle and no messengers.

Then, like a gambler down to his last few chips, the Jehovah's Witnesses laid it all on the line and declared that 1975 would be the end of the world.[49] And if you were holding your breath to find out if the world ended in 1975, rest assured, it did not. Just another failed prediction in a long span of failed predictions. Ron Rhodes explains the disappointments of many of the organization's members in the years following 1975, by stating that "hundreds of thousands of Jehovah's Witnesses left the Watchtower organization worldwide between 1976 and 1978."[50] After the decline in membership, the Jehovah's Witnesses had apparently learned their lesson.

The Rejection of the Cross

To Christians, the Cross is a sign and symbol of the sacrificial and atoning death of Jesus Christ for sinners (Col 1:20). However, to the members of the Watch Tower Society, they reject the Cross; the organization explains:

> Nowhere does the Bible suggest that the earliest Christians used the cross as a religious symbol. Instead, it was the Romans of that era who used the cross design to symbolize *their* gods. Then, about 300 years after Jesus' death, Roman Emperor Constantine adopted the cross as the emblem of his armies, and it thereafter became associated with the "Christian" church.[51]

Professor of Theology Robin Jensen counters the claim by stating, "There is no evidence that Christians intentionally borrowed the cross from pre-Christian cultic symbols."[52]

LESSONS IN WOLFOLOGY

1. NEW HERESY IS OFTEN JUST OLD HERESY WITH A MAKEOVER.

It is mostly incidental that ancient Arianism has common ground with the Jehovah's Witnesses. However, they do share a rigid literalism that led them to adopt similar points of view. What I am getting at here is that there really is not a whole lot of new heresy. For 2,000 years, the church has wrestled with many controversies and unorthodox movements. So, when something "new" comes along it is most likely a retread of something the church has already dealt with in the past. The ancient Montanists come alive in the Church of Jesus Christ of Latter-day Saints of today. The ancient Sabellian lives on through Oneness Pentecostalism. Ancient Arianism has had a rebirth in the Jehovah's Witnesses. There is hardly ever anything new about heresy.

2. BIBLICAL CHRISTOLOGY IS A CORNERSTONE OF ORTHODOXY THAT CANNOT BE COMPROMISED.

Who is Jesus? The nature of Jesus's person and work is a fundamental question for all people: to the Christian, to the unbeliever, and to those trapped in false religious movements. According to the Watch Tower Society:

- Jesus was the angel Michael in his preexistence. Implication? Jesus is not co-eternal with God the Father. Jesus may be more than man, but he is always less than God in the modern Arian-Jehovah's Witnesses.

- In the *New World Translation* (Jehovah's Witnesses' version of the Bible), John 1:1 teaches that Jesus was *a god*. This is a further denial of the deity of Christ as well as the Holy Trinity.

- Jesus was born merely as a man, through the force power of the Holy Spirit. Not only is this a rejection of Jesus's full deity, it is a rejection of the divine nature of the Holy Spirit as well.

- The Cross of Jesus Christ, which figures prominently into the centrality of the Gospel of Christ (1 Cor 1:18; Heb 12:2; Phil 2:8) is intentionally minimized by the Watch Tower Society.

- Jesus's bodily resurrection (Mk 16:1-7; Mt 28:5-6) is also rejected by the Jehovah's Witnesses.

David Scaer has expressed quite powerfully that "all theology is Christology."[53] Scaer explains what he means by the phrase, stating, "Christology is the overarching category under which theology, that is, our knowledge of God, is to be placed."[54]

What is at stake for the Christian is summarized by Sinclair Ferguson, who wrote:

> Does it really matter if those views are wrong, indeed heretical, so long as we know that Jesus saves and we witness to others about Him? After all, the important thing is that we preach the gospel.
>
> But that is precisely the point—Jesus Christ Himself is the gospel. Like loose threads in a tapestry—pull on any of these views, and the entire gospel will unravel. If the Christ we trust and preach is not qualified to save us, we have a false Christ.[55]

If we misunderstand who Jesus is, we will miss the Gospel entirely.

3. THE CHURCH IS NOT ONLY CALLED TO DEFEND THE TRUTH, BUT WE'RE ALSO CALLED TO SHARE THE TRUTH.

Sadly, I have heard Christians say terrible things about both the Jehovah's Witnesses and the Latter-day Saints because they brought their brand of religion to their doorsteps. But I have spoken to several Jehovah's Witnesses and LDS missionaries throughout my years of following Christ, and what I have found is that most of them are kind, caring, and considerate. They have such convictions about what they believe that they persistently share their views in a world where it has increasingly become more and more taboo.

Now what I am about to say may hurt a little, so buckle up and brace for impact. There is a boldness that I have seen in members of false religions that is sometimes lacking in Evangelical Christianity. It is bewildering, to say the least. When I was in Bible college, I had an Old Testament professor, Charlie Draper, who would sometimes challenge his students by saying: "You know, the Mormons go knocking on doors all the time. That's because it works. You should try it some-time." While Evangelical Protestant denominations are either stagnant or in decline, the Jehovah's Witnesses continue to show modest growth.[56] Baptist minister Walter Martin once asked, "Are we willing to do for the truth what others are willing to do for a lie?"[57]

4. A KEY MARK OF A FALSE PROPHET IS THAT THEY MAKE FALSE PROPHECIES.

False prophets make false predictions. The Scriptures say to pay attention to those who claim to speak for God but obviously do not. For example, Lamentations 2:14, "Your prophets have seen for you false and deceptive visions; they have not exposed your iniquity to re-store your fortunes, but have seen for your oracles that are false and misleading." Or Jeremiah 23:14, "I did not send the prophets, yet they ran; I did not speak to them, yet they prophesied."

Over the course of 100 years, the Jehovah's Witnesses made no less than five predictions that Christ would return and that history would enter its final crescendo. I have always found it interesting that Jesus said of Himself, "But concerning that day and hour no one knows, not even the angels of heaven, nor the Son, but the Father only (Mt 24:36)," yet, there are men and women who have claimed through-out the ages to have a better sense of the end of history than Jesus. I can hear the late R.C. Sproul's response to these prognosticators, "What's wrong with you people?"[58]

Liberalism on the one hand and the religion of the historic church on the other are not two varieties of the same religion, but two distinct religions proceeding from altogether separate roots.

—J. Gresham Machen, *Christianity and Liberalism*

Mainline Protestant Liberalism

My son is almost 14 years old, and he is a strapping young man. For his age, he is in the top two percent of people for height; at nearly six feet tall he towers me. But the truth is, he has always been tall. Even when he was a toddler, he was bigger than most of the other kids. However, when he started playing soccer at the ripe old age of four, he used his size advantage to knock kids down the way a bowling ball knocks down pins (oh, the humanity—who would have ever thought you would see blood and guts like that at the local YMCA soccer league?).

To say that my son was overly aggressive at that age is an understatement (I blame his mother). The look of disgust on the parents of the other kids that my son had just knocked limp to the ground caused my wife and me to put on sunglasses and slink into our lawn chairs. The problem was that our son had just not learned *the fundamentals*. He did not understand the mechanics of passing, kicking, defending. He understood competitiveness, but he did not yet comprehend the basics of the sport.

Since that time, he developed into a solid defender and played the game for several years until falling in love with basketball (he is six feet tall, after all) and is now learning the fundamentals of that sport as well. Every game has fundamental tenets: in karate, you must learn how to take a fall; in football, you must learn how to tackle correctly, or you might hurt your neck; and in golf, you must keep your eye on the ball and follow through with your swing. Well, as with sports, *Christianity has fundamentals, too.*

The fundamentals of the Christian faith are the things that make Christianity what it is. Take away the fundamental teaching of the Bible, and you will lose Christianity. Think about it like this: a house has fundamental characteristics, like a footer, a foundation, and a roof. There are secondary things that make up a house, too, such as windows, drywall, and an HVAC system. Now, secondary materials are essential, but if you take away a home's footer, foundation, or roof, the house is incomplete. Well, that is sort of what *Mainline Protestant Liberalism* (MPL) is. It is something that believes itself to be a version of Christianity, but in truth, it is sub-Christianity. Or, like what I mentioned above—it is an incomplete Christianity. Let us find out why.

HISTORY

In the 2,000 years of Christian history, MPL is a newer development that began in the 19th century. Like most other philosophical and theological movements, MPL is a result of a synthesis of philosophies; one part the Enlightenment, and one part Rationalism. Both Enlightenment and Rationalism focused on individualism, reason, science, and skepticism. As Roman Catholicism suffered a loss of powers in the 16th century, the Enlightenment created an awakening. It was like pouring boiling water into an ice-cold-glass—it shattered into a hundred different pieces, going in all directions. The religious oppression and authoritarianism of the institutional church gave way to the autonomy of the individual. These were all precursors to the sea of changes that would occur over the next 300 hundred years, like the American and French Revolutions of the 18th century, the industrial revolution of the 19th century, as well as the decline of biblical supernaturalism.

Liberal Theologians and Seminaries

Friedrich Schleiermacher (1768-1834) was one of the earliest theological innovators (a polite way of saying rejecting Scripture as an authority) in applying enlightenment-skepticism to the realm of theology and hermeneutics. Schleiermacher's theology was primarily concerned with man's inner being. Put differently, individuals became enlightened through Jesus, in whom God's consciousness had been perfected. Now, if this sounds psychological, it is because it was explicitly meant to be that way. Sociologist John S. Knox explained that Schleiermacher's "innovative interpretations and theories were quite culturally influential and began a push toward a more relaxed, more creative understanding of Christianity, whose influence can still be seen in contemporary theology and culture."[1]

Schleiermacher's ideas had a far-reaching effect. Chief among them was the methodology of *Higher Criticism*. Higher criticism seeks to determine the sources of the biblical text, the historical origins and reliability of the Scriptures, and the assumptions of its authors. This approach to the Scriptures along with other streams of thought that developed in the 18th century primed the pump for anti-supernaturalism, especially as Charles Darwin's *The Origin of Species* (1859) arrived on the scene.

Darwin's theory upset the applecart of Christian creationism. Darwin's premise was that organisms change over time to adapt to their environment because of their innate survival instincts.[2] Thus, the earth had to be much older than the prevailing opinion of the church. Evolution must have taken millions of years to create as many distinct and diverse creatures who were once a part of the primordial ooze. Indeed, Darwin's theory first crawled, then it grew legs and picked up speed and gained a foothold in universities and seminaries.

Berlin in the middle of the 19th century was the proverbial launch pad for theological Liberalism.[3] It influenced significant theological movements and denominations (both in Europe and North America). The Berlin School took Schleiermacher's higher critical methods and infused his skepticism with Darwinian evolution. The net result was that mankind had finally transcended the superstitions of its past. This way of thinking saw the Bible as an ancient text like any other ancient work, *simply a man-made work of fiction.*[4]

Liberalism was arguing the church must adapt to modern times by removing the supernaturalism of the Bible. Many scholars believe that Christianity must first appeal to modern man's sensibilities to remain relevant. This philosophy made its way from the minds of the philosophers into the seminaries and the church. One example is that of Charles Briggs (1841-1913). A Presbyterian theologian, Briggs trained in higher critical methods in Berlin and ended up planting anti-supernaturalism both at Union Theological Seminary and by proximity the Presbyterian Church (PCUSA).[5] Briggs was excommunicated in 1893 for his rejection of *sola scriptura*, but not without first striking at the heart of old-school orthodoxy.[6]

However, Briggs was just the first salvo in what would become a massive takeover of several American seminaries. Union, Yale, Princeton, and Harvard divinity schools would all succumb to higher criticism and embrace liberalism. It was a domino effect. Soon, denominations would fall. High church Presbyterianism became a victim of its penchant for intellectualism and reasonableness, the miracles of the Bible no longer held sway. The theological components of this new spirituality did not stay isolated in the ivory tower of the academic world but instead soon found their way into prominent pulpit ministries.

Demythologizing and Bultmann

Rudolf Bultmann (1884-1976) was a Lutheran scholar who had advanced the higher critical method, building on Schleiermacher's work (as well as the scholarship of those at the University of Tübingen, like Baur, Strauss, and Feuerbach). He proposed a solution to the threats of Darwinism and modernity to Christianity. Bultmann reasoned that

Christianity, with its blood atonement, virgin birth, and resurrections, needed to adapt itself to the age of science.

Bultmann's plan was distinct from outright Liberalism, which sought to reject supernatural elements of Scripture outright; instead, Bultmann focused on *Demythologizing* the Word of God.[7] This was Bultmann's attempt to take the "alien-world-picture," like the ancient world that the Bible was written in, and make it a "familiar one" which is sensible to modern man.[8] Furthermore, Bultmann's interpretive approach was driven by "pastoral concern."[9] Bultmann's interpretation of the mythical portions of Scriptures was driven by two things: first, getting man to come to a real understanding of himself; and second, helping man to take the right actions.[10]

The Orators of the Liberal Movement

With the anti-supernaturalism of liberal higher criticism firmly in place, it left its own share of problems. *After all, what does a minister preach if the Bible has been emptied of the fundamentals of Christianity?* For the preachers who came out of divinity schools compromised by the rejection of ancient orthodoxy, problems soon surfaced. For example, how does a minister apply texts like Jesus walking on water, or Jesus raising Lazarus from the dead, or Jesus causing the blind to see? With supernaturalism left behind, it was left to men like Charles Monroe Sheldon (1857-1946), Walter Rauschenbusch (1861-1918), and Harry Emerson Fosdick (1878-1969) to make the Liberal gospel heard.

Primarily, the preachers of this movement focused on the construction of a Christian society removed from the divine elements of the Bible. This humanistic Christianity was concerned with the plight of real injustices, while their conservative fundamentalist counterparts were still blabbering on about blood-sacrifices, hell, and healings. Liberals believed they were offering the modern world a relevant religion that could upend the way of life in the Jim Crow South, end poverty and world hunger, and fix the inequalities of the capitalistic economic system.

Furthermore, Liberal proponents viewed preaching as a blend of spirituality and psychology. Consider the emphasis of Rev. Joseph F. Flint, who happily welcomed the psychological focus of preaching as far back as 1899. Flint wrote:

A significant sign of the times is the widespread conviction that specific radical changes should be made in the curriculum of our divinity schools. Among other things, a prominent place is to be assigned to psychology. This is a fortunate choice. The new study of applied psychology once thoroughly understood and intelligently practiced, will of itself accomplish wonders. It means the transfer of emphasis from the world of books to the world of men, from the abstract to the concrete, and from the speculative to the practical.[11]

Pastoral students in MPL seminaries were being trained to become quasi-therapists on a mass level. Preaching became primarily about meeting *the real needs of man*, as well as *the real duties of man*.

It would be the novels of Charles Monroe Sheldon that promoted the idea of Jesus as the supreme moral example for mankind to follow; especially in terms of seeking a just society. Sheldon was using his popular spiritual tales to promote what would become known as the *Social Gospel* movement. Most important was Sheldon's work, *In His Steps* (1896); it was subtitled *What would Jesus do?* It was this book that catapulted MPL as it sold an astounding 50,000,000 copies worldwide.[12] Likewise, Sheldon inspired other notable voices in the social gospel movement. None was more important than Walter Rauschenbusch.

Rauschenbusch had envisioned the kingdom of God operating to bring about social reformation.[13] Rauschenbusch, an avowed socialist, would further advance the concepts that were present in the writings of Sheldon. Rauschenbusch was a zealous social reformer/preacher. He sought to bring awareness to the public conscience to issues like adolescent poverty, malnutrition, crime, and disease. Rauschenbusch articulated that Christ was a social and religious *emancipator*, stating that "Jesus saw his mission in raising to free and full life those whom life had held down and hurt."[14] However, it was Harry Emerson Fosdick who became most vocal in his detestation of what we know as evangelical Christianity (or *the Fundamentalists*).

Fosdick, the preaching pastor of Riverside Church in Manhattan, crystalized the battle lines with his famous sermon "Shall the Fundamentalists Win?" This is one of the most famous sermons of the early 20th century and easily accessible for today's readers. In the sermon, Fosdick critiques Christian Fundamentalism for their dogmatism. Famously, Fosdick proclaimed:

> It is interesting to note where the Fundamentalists are driving in their stakes to mark out the deadline of doctrine around the church, across which no one is to pass except on terms of agreement. They insist that we must all believe in the historicity of certain special miracles, preeminently the virgin birth of our Lord; that we must believe in special theory of inspiration—that the original documents of the Scripture, which of course we no longer possess, were inerrantly dictated to men a good deal as a man might dictate to a stenographer; that we must believe in the special theory of the atonement—that the blood of our Lord, shed in a substitutionary death, placates an alienated Deity and makes possible welcome for the returning sinner; and that we must believe in the second coming of our Lord upon the clouds of heaven to set up a millennium here, as the only way in which God can bring history to a worthy denouement. Such are some of the stakes which are being driven, marking a deadline of doctrine around the church.[15]

Fosdick fumed against the doctrinal boundaries that the Fundamentalists created. But for the Fundamentalists, Christianity was wrapped up in the supernaturalism of Jesus's life and ministry. To reject the virgin birth or the resurrection is not like getting your order wrong at *Applebee's*; instead, it is a complete denial of Christianity.

FUNDAMENTALISM STRIKES BACK
R. A. Torrey

Fundamentalism did not take the influx of MPL lying down. No, they shot back both theologically and institutionally. Theologically, the prowess of men like R. A. Torrey, B. B. Warfield, G. Campbell Morgan, and Charles Erdman (64 contributors in all) forged together the famous work—*The Fundamentals: A Testimony to Truth* (1917). In this twelve-volume set, a cohort of conservative Bible teachers and scholars defined the non-negotiable doctrines (the fundamentals) of the Christian faith. Overall, *The Fundamentals* was 90 essays that were primarily concerned with repudiating liberalism within Christianity (though it defended against other challenges too, like Mormonism and Roman Catholicism). The work is recognized as a clarion call to the conservative church to awaken to the existential threat of higher criticism.

Torrey was a towering figure in the early Fundamentalist movement. An 1878 Yale Divinity School graduate, Torrey became instrumental in the formation of Bible institutes. Torrey helped D. L. Moody establish the Moody Bible Institute in Chicago through 1889-1906. Then Torrey did the heavy lifting in the creation of a new Bible school in Los Angeles named Bible Institute of Los Angeles (now Biola) in 1912. The rise of Bible institutes were themselves meant to be a protest of the higher criticism in what had once been Evangelical seminaries.

Most importantly, Torrey had placed his finger on the main issues confronting Christianity in the West. Consider what Torrey wrote in his work, *The Fundamentals of Christianity* (1918), that "the position held by so many today, that the Bible is a good book, perhaps the best book in the world, but at the same time it is full of errors that must be corrected by the higher wisdom of our day, is utterly illogical and absolutely ridiculous. If the Bible is not what it claims to be, it is a fraud—an outrageous fraud."[16]

J. Gresham Machen

As higher criticism made its way into the mainline denominations, a fracture began to occur. The PCUSA was the first to feel the division as the Orthodox Presbyterian church emerged as a response to the encroachment of Liberalism in 1936.[17] J. Gresham Machen (1881-1937) spear-headed conservative opposition in the Presbyterian sphere. Machen was a zealous Reformed warrior, a storehouse of Princetonian theology, the kind made famous by Charles Hodge and B. B. Warfield. When Princeton was lost to liberalism, Machen counted the cost and paid it. The net result was the founding of Westminster Theological Seminary in 1929.[18]

Furthermore, Machen had the aptitude to take on his liberal opponents. This is most exemplified in his work *Christianity and Liberalism* (1923). Machen understood that Christianity and liberalism were not compatible, and were set against each other as much as orange juice and toothpaste—they simply did not mix well together. Machen made this observation, "The chief modern rival of Christianity is 'liberalism.' An examination of the teachings of liberalism in comparison with those of Christianity will show that at every point, the two movements are in direct opposition."[19] Machen rightly acknowledged that "Christian-Liberalism" was an oxymoron. They were incompatible.

THE RISE OF THE NEW EVANGELICALS
Ockenga and Friends

Out of the newly formed Westminster Theological Seminary came one of Machen's brightest and capable students, Harold Ockenga (1905-1985). Ockenga was raised with a holiness pietism and had been fiercely committed to the service of Christ from a young age.[20] Ockenga's devotion to Christ could be seen in his dedication to becoming the most capable theologian and academic he could. After his graduation at Taylor University, Ockenga entered Princeton Theological Seminary in 1927, at the height of the Fundamentalist-Liberal controversy.[21] It was there that he came under the tutelage of Machen. Eventually, when Machen established Westminster in 1929, Ockenga migrated to be with Machen in the new seminary. Graduating in 1930, Ockenga set a course that would shape the Evangelical world for the next fifty years.

Ockenga represented the most excellent scholarship among conservative Christianity. Alongside him would come Carl F. H. Henry.

The two would become close counterparts and would be the leading voices of Bible-believing intellectualism. Henry, who had earned two PhDs from separate institutions by age 36, would write *The Uneasy Conscience of Modern Fundamentalism* in 1947. This work offered a critique of both MPL and rigid Christian Fundamentalism. Both Ockenga and Henry were representative of the new wave of Evangelical Christian scholars who could compete with the scholarship of the most educated liberal scholars, but do so from the position of a firm belief in the inerrancy and authority of Scripture. On this voyage men like George Eldon Ladd, Merrill Tenney, and Gleason Archer represented the best of Evangelical intellectualism.

Under the guidance of Ockenga (and with the financial backing of the evangelist Charles Fuller), Fuller Theological Seminary was established in 1947. Set in Pasadena, California, it was to be the repository of the best conservative Christian scholarship; a base of operations to counter theological Liberalism, and also engage the culture in ways that fundamentalism had rejected. What Westminster had become to the East Coast, Fuller was to become to the West Coast; an evangelical academy that would train and equip believers with a "fresh intellectual defense of Christianity built on rigorous scholarship."[22]

ASSESSMENTS

Liberalism had basically won the battle in the seminaries. Practically every major theological institution had adopted higher criticism. Even denominationally controlled institutions like the Southern Baptist Theological Seminary (Southern Baptist Convention), McCormick Theological Seminary (PCUSA), and Luther Seminary (American Lutheran Church) were not immune to modernity's invasion. Fundamentalists had withdrawn to create their own Christian sub-culture—separatism became their strategy. Many modern Fundamentalists have become characterized by rabid loyalties to Dispensationalism, the King James Bible, and a strict bias against Christian intellectualism.

Eventually, more denominations would fracture towards the middle of the 20th century as the tension between long-held Christian convictions and modernity were unable to co-exist. The Civil Rights movement, led by Martin Luther King, Jr., emerged during the 1960s. The movement was positively fueled by the Social Gospel and brought about the much-needed transformation that Sheldon, Rauschenbusch, and Fosdick had hoped.

Nevertheless, robbed of true spirituality centered upon the Word of God, MPL began to sharply decline. For example, in 1965, the PCUSA had a membership total of 3.3 million members. By 2012, that number has fallen to 1.85 million, a decline of 44 percent over the course of almost 50 years.[23] However, the Southern Baptist Convention, over that same course of time grew from 10.8 million to 15.8 million, a 46 percent increase in membership.[24] *Why?* Sociologist, Benton Johnson pointed out 35 years ago that the primary issue was *relevance.* Johnson explained, "If the liberal churches are to recover their strength and cultural influence, they will have to make liberal Christianity more *relevant and compelling* to their own constituency."[25] The paradox is plain. MPL, in trying to be relevant to modern man, abandoned the authority of the Bible. In doing so, MPL effectively became irrelevant. MPL attempted to save Christianity and discovered to its own chagrin, that biblical Christianity didn't need saving at all.

Is MPL dead? No. But, it is weakened. MPL is like *Jadis the Queen of Charn*, she may die in *The Lion, the Witch, and the Wardrobe*, but she shows up in different iterations. That is what MPL does. It has the same basic problems found in new manifestations. MPL rejects the authority of Scripture, denies the supernatural, and is primarily concerned with social issues. In the 1960s it was the Civil Rights movement; in the 1970s and 1980s it was the push for feminist-egalitarianism; in the 2000's it was *Red Letter Christianity; The Emerging Church* spanned several decades but died out by 2008. Right now, some believe that MPL has been resurrected in the *Woke Christian* movement. However, I think it is too early to tell. For whatever reason, MPL just won't stay dead.

LESSONS IN WOLFOLOGY

1. THE THREE PILLARS OF *SOLA SCRIPTURA*: BIBLICAL INSPIRATION, BIBLICAL INERRANCY, AND BIBLICAL INFALLIBILITY.

Can we trust the Bible? That's the question at the center of the debates between Christianity and MPL. Helpful to a Christian's understanding are the three pillars of *Sola Scriptura* (Scripture alone is sufficient for leading the church in what she is to believe and how she is to act). First, *Biblical Inspiration*. Biblical inspiration means that God has delivered His revealed will through holy men in the ancient past. God so worked through the personalities of men like Moses, David, the Prophets, and the Apostles to communicate His word exactly as He intended it to be. 2nd Timothy 3:16 says, "All Scripture is breathed out by God and profitable for teaching, for reproof, for correction, and for training in righteousness, that the man of God may be complete, equipped for every good work." So, the writers of Scripture were not brain-dead automatons, rather God used the individual nature of each writer to convey His revelation to mankind.

Next, is *Biblical Inerrancy*. Norman Geisler explains what we mean by inerrancy this way. He states, "The Bible is inspired but is it inerrant, that is without errors? The reason for a positive answer is simple: The Bible is the Word of God, and God cannot err; therefore, the Bible cannot err. To deny the inerrancy of the Bible one must either affirm that God can err or else that the Bible is not the Word of God."[26] What God reveals to us in the Bible is true without any mixture of error. The Bible is unlike any other book in the world. We read the Bible, but the Bible also reads us; we seek to get to the heart of the Bible, but the Bible gets to our heart; the Bible is not a textbook, it is a living book.

Lastly, *Biblical Infallibility* means that Scripture is the ultimate authority of a believer's life. The Bible does not teach us how to make pancakes or fix hydraulic tanks, or how to polish a pair of old leather shoes. The Bible does not teach those things because that is not the

Bible's goal. Instead, the Scriptures were written so that we would know exactly what God wants us to believe, do, and obey.

2. THE CHRISTIAN GOSPEL IS RELEVANT REGARDLESS OF THE OPINIONS OF THE BROADER CULTURE.

MPL sort of reminds me of a 9th grader who wants to sit at the A-list table during second period lunch. They want to wear the right clothes, listen to the right music, and say the right things—obsessed with acceptance. Of course, as it has already been pointed out—the great undoing of MPL is that in jettisoning historic Christianity, they have become irrelevant to the world around them. Christianity is a strange religion, filled with blood and lepers; of men who get swallowed by fish and live to tell about it; of miracles and demons. Yep, it is strange, but it is also true.

If you take the perspective that you can ever make biblical Christianity, filled with all its supernatural elements, palpable to the unbelieving community, then you should call me to talk about some oceanfront property I have in Arizona (God bless George Strait). Instead, believers should embrace the peculiarities of this ancient faith of ours and proclaim it to the world. The most relevant truths anyone can hear today are the timeless truths of Jesus' gospel. At the end of the day, a world blinded by the darkness of sin needs the church's light (Mt 5:16).

3. CHRISTIANITY NEEDS TO BE DEFENDED, BUT CHRISTIANITY NEVER NEEDS TO BE RESCUED.

This brief excursus shows us that we should be extremely grateful for those godly men and women who came before us to contend for the faith. It also confirms that *Christianity needs defending, but it never needs to be rescued.* Liberalism wanted to save Christianity from the dangers of modernity. MPL thought it could remove the foundations of Christianity and it would survive. It makes about as much sense as severing one's head because they have developed a migraine. Liberalism's rejection of inerrancy led the movement to reject the very essence of biblical Christianity.

For what does it profit a man to gain the whole world and forfeit his soul?

—Jesus, Mark 8:36

The Prosperity Gospel

America. The land of opportunity and liberty. Freedom and success are traits associated with what those in the United States call *The American Dream*. The American Dream is simple: success comes to those who are willing to work hard and play by the rules. Unsurprisingly, the American Dream also has its own sort of religious makings in what has come to be known as *The Prosperity Gospel*. That is not to say that the American Dream is terrible, just that others have co-opted the realization of that dream and attached a sub-Christian meaning to it. Sort of like the hotdog that has been staying warm on the rollers over at the local gas station. It is undoubtedly not the hotdog one could have hoped for, but with enough ketchup, mustard, and relish, you can get it down. The Prosperity Gospel is like that. A weak and anemic version of Christianity made appealing not only by the way that it looks but also by what it promises.

But what exactly is the Prosperity Gospel? Costi Hinn provides clarity to the meaning of the prosperity movement; he says, "A very basic definition of the prosperity gospel can be described this way: God's plan is for you to *live your best life now*. Health, wealth, and happiness are guaranteed on earth for all who follow Jesus. Heaven is simply the eternal extension of your temporal blessings."[1] *But where does this movement come from?* Modern prosperity teaching is a culmination of mind power spiritualism that has been built on the backs of several vital religious leaders from the mid-19th century to the present day. In the proceeding pages, we will explore the development of the Prosperity Gospel through the lives of the movement's significant proponents.

EARLY KEY LEADERS
Phineas Quimby

Phineas Parkhurst Quimby (1802-1866) can hardly be called a Christian; instead, he was a transcendentalist of the early 19th century. Quimby held great animus towards religious organizations. A native of New Hampshire, Quimby came under the influence of the metaphysical teachings of the great New England minds of Emerson, Thoreau, and Melville. Furthermore, Quimby adopted the techniques of German physician Franz Anton Mesmer (1734-1815).[2] Mesmer developed a pseudo-science known as *Animal Magnetism* which he believed was "a universal force of living beings with the capability of producing physical effects over the matter, in particular, healing."[3]

Quimby, under the inspiration of the transcendentalism of Mesmer, firmly believed that the mind had the power to heal the body of physical infirmities. Quimby became known as "Doctor" to many in the New England region for his psychotherapeutic approach to helping the sick cure themselves through the power of cognition. Quimby practiced "New Thought" spiritual and mental healing; clairvoyance and hypnotism became the primary tools of his trade.[4]

A Deist, Quimby believed that humanity had been created by a divine creator who was removed from the affairs of humankind. However, because of the divine origins of humanity, Quimby assumed that man was "quintessentially divine and perfectly healthy, as an idea in the Creative Mind [of God]—as healthy, say, like a tree in a good environment; that man's mind is creative, and if it harbors ugly thoughts, will create an ugly, diseased body."[5] In other words, *change the way your mind thinks, and the body will follow.* Likewise, the words one speaks can alter the mind, thus affecting the body. Quimby's influence was far-reaching. His teachings would not only personally affect Mary Baker

Eddy's life, but inspired her to create the religious sect, Christian Science. However, Quimby's ideas take Christian form in the teachings of E.W. Kenyon, Oral Roberts, and Norman Vincent Peale.

E. W. Kenyon

Essek William Kenyon (1867-1948), like Quimby before him, was a New Englander. However, Kenyon grew up working poor and did not come to faith in Christ until his later teenage years. Converted as a Methodist, Kenyon would be considered by many to be the architect of the "Word of Faith" movement. Educated at Emerson College in Boston, Kenyon came under the influence of "New Thought" teaching and the Christian Science of Eddy.[6] Though not technically a Pentecostal, Kenyon would wield incredible influence over the rise of the Pentecostal movement, especially in the case of faith healing crusades.

Emphasizing the Quimbian principles he learned at Emerson College, Kenyon dressed the skeleton of "New Thought" with the skin of Christianity. For example, Kenyon explains:

> The believer does not need to ask the Father to heal him when he is sick, because 'Surely he hath borne our sickness and carried our diseases; yet we did esteem him stricken, smitten of God and afflicted.' God laid our diseases on Jesus. Isaiah 53:10 states that it pleased Jehovah to make Him sick with our sicknesses so that by His stripes, we are healed. If we are healed, then we do not need to pray for our healing. All we need to do is rebuke the enemy in Jesus' Name…It is all so simple.[7]

Interestingly, Kenyon was not a prominent figure in his own day and time. Kenyon's legacy would instead live on through Kenneth Hagin.

Kenneth Hagin

Kenneth Hagin (1917-2003) was a prominent faith healer among the Charismatic movement throughout the 20th century. Texas-born and Baptist bred, Hagin began a ministry that focused on spiritual gifts like healing, visions, and speaking in tongues. Unfettered from his Baptist roots, Hagin adopted Pentecostalism's spiritual vibrancy. Like Kenyon before him, Hagin emphasized "the power of believers voicing their beliefs with the same authority as the Scriptures."[8] Hagin's ministry took off during the 1960s as people gravitated to his brand; by 1974, Hagin launched a successful radio program, started the Rhema Bible Training Center, and captivated thousands through his faith healing crusades. Hagin looms large as the first major icon of the Word of Faith movement, only rivaled by Oral Roberts.

Oral Roberts

Oral Roberts (1918-2009) became a spiritual dynamo in the 1950s and had tremendous success for decades following. Roberts gained his following through his tent crusades and the national press he received when NBC began to broadcast his revivals. Roberts, in many ways, was the forerunner and precursor to the prosperity-televangelists that became prominent in the 1980s. Ordained into the Pentecostal Holiness movement, Roberts eventually adopted the United Methodist (UMC) denomination as his home. However, Roberts remained centrally focused on the work of the Holy Spirit, faith healing, and Charismatic issues. Central to Roberts' legacy is the university that he established in his hometown of Tulsa, Oklahoma, in 1963.

A key concept of his teaching was *Seed-Faith*. This concept borrows the biblical metaphor of "sowing and reaping" and turns it into a spiritual rewards program. Roberts taught that "personal prosperity was endorsed by God."[9] This way of thought was also critical to funding Roberts' life, ministry, and university as well. The teaching caught on through Roberts' book *The Miracle of Seed-Faith* (1974). The book distilled Roberts' seed-faith in three easily discernable principles: first, "God is your source"; second, "Give that it may be given to you"; and third, "Expect a miracle."

Though Roberts' ministry and success were lauded throughout the 1960s and 70s, there were a host of controversies and personal tragedies that befell him. Roberts alleged in 1987 that the Lord would bring his life to an end if he did not raise eight million dollars in funding.[10] Additionally, Roberts publicly claimed that the Lord had revealed to him that a cure for cancer was near. Roberts leveraged these claims to fund a medical and cancer research center.

Norman Vincent Peale

In 1898, just a little south east of Dayton in the town of Bowersville, Ohio, was born Norman Vincent Peale. Reared in the Methodist tradition, Peale attended both Ohio Wesleyan and the Boston University School of Theology. Soon after, Peale went from the humble beginnings of an obscure town in Ohio to multiple congregations in New York where he would, by every human metric, navigate one of the most successful ministries in the 20th century. Peale is most notable for his teaching on *the power of positive thinking*. Peale reasoned, "The positive thinker... sends out positive thoughts, together with vital images of hope, optimism and creativity. He, therefore, activates the world around him positively and strongly tends to draw back to himself positive results."[11] To say it differently, the power of one's mind has the ability to shape and mold their environment to net helpful outcomes.

Peale came to national prominence in 1935 through his weekly radio broadcast *The Art of Living* and several best-selling books on positive thinking and personal success. Under the garb of classic Christian teaching, Peale advanced a religious form of self-improvement that would be most manifest in the ministries of Robert Schuller and Joel Osteen.

THE TELEVANGELISM BOOM
Paul and Jan Crouch

The medium of television carved out new pathways for the Charismatic movement. This was especially the case through the life and ministry of Paul and Jan Crouch, the co-founders of the Trinity Broadcasting Network (TBN). Paul and Jan met at Evangel College in the 1950s and were subsequently married in 1957. In 1973, the Crouch family along with Jim Bakker embarked on turning a "low watt UHF station in Santa Ana, California…into a global, Christian network."[12]

The platform that TBN has given to the modern Charismatic movement cannot be underestimated. With a global reach of 2 billion homes, TBN has promoted teachers like Paula White, Kenneth Copeland, and T. D. Jakes and helped them garner worldwide attention. Additionally, TBN has helped pave the way for other broadcast networks that further the health and wealth ideologies, like Victory Channel, Daystar, and God TV. Years ago, John MacArthur pointed out:

> TBN is by far the leading perpetrator of that [prosperity teaching] lie worldwide. Virtually all the network's main celebrities tell listeners that God will give them healing, wealth, and other material blessings in return for their money. On program, after program people are urged to "plant a seed" by sending "the largest bill you have or the biggest check you can write" with the promise that God will miraculously make them rich in return. That same message dominates all of TBN's major fundraising drives.[13]

Jim and Tammy Faye Bakker

During the 1970s and through the 1980s, Jim and Tammy Faye Bakker became "Christian" celebrities through the success of their show *The PTL Club* (The Praise the Lord Club). The couple met at North Central University in 1960 and were married the following year. They desired to be in full-time ministry as evangelists. The two got their start doing a variety show on the Christian Broadcasting Network in 1966. By 1973, Jim and Tammy Faye came alongside Paul and Jan

Crouch to create TBN. In 1976 they launched *The PTL Club* and grew a tremendous following that was generously funded by millions of dollars they received in support from their viewing audience. *The PTL Club* was a Christianized version of late-night shows of the time, featuring prominent Christian voices and other Christian celebrities.

The popularity of the couple grew to epic proportions throughout the 1980s but so did their spending habits. Jim Bakker said once, "God wants his people to go first-class," which is precisely what he and his wife, Tammy Faye, did. Lavish vacations, shopping addiction, and expensive cars were the hallmarks of the lifestyle that Jim and Tammy Faye cultivated. All the while, viewership believed the Bakkers to be upstanding Christian leaders who embodied the tropes of victory preaching: God loves you and has a plan for your life; pull out your inner-winner; give, and you will get.

By 1987, the kingdom that the Bakkers had built came crashing to the ground. Jim Bakker had found himself at the center of a terrible sex scandal. These allegations stirred up the IRS to take a closer look at some fraud that they had perceived to be at work in *The PTL Club* ministries reaching back to 1985. The IRS uncovered over a million dollars of fraud that Jim Bakker had committed under the guise of religious purposes. Bakker had funneled funds from the tax-exempt ministry to use them for the couple's personal home. Furthermore, the fundraising activities of *The PTL Club* from 1984 to 1987 had become the grounds for indictment. Jim Bakker was sentenced to 8 years in prison. In 1993, Tammy Faye filed for divorce from Jim.

When Bakker was released from prison in 1996, he repudiated his affiliation with the prosperity movement in his book *I Was Wrong*. Bakker stated:

> However, I had to admit that the prosperity message did not line up with the tenor of Scripture. My heart was crushed to think that I led so many people astray. I was appalled that I could have been so wrong, and I was deeply grateful that God had not struck me dead as a false prophet.[14]

Bakker has since become more focused on apocalypticism through his daytime show—*The Jim Bakker Show*—a program that is geared towards doomsday preparation. However, chicanery remains. For example, in the wake of the Covid-19 crisis, Bakker has been accused of hawking products that he claimed could "cure, eliminate, or deactivate Coronavirus."[15]

Kenneth Copeland

Born in 1936, Kenneth Copeland is one of the most prominent voices in the prosperity movement. Copeland developed a unique set of skills through his early adulthood. In 1957, he used his vocal talents for a song that went gold ("Pledge of Love"). In 1959, he became a commercial pilot. After becoming a Christian in the early 1960s, he desired to enter vocational ministry. Subsequently, Copeland went to Oral Roberts University, where he became a close acquaintance of Roberts, serving as Roberts' pilot and chauffeur. The seed-faith teaching that was central to Oral Roberts became the cornerstone of Copeland's ministry.

Worth between an estimated 300 to 750 million dollars, Copeland has amassed his fortune through his *Kenneth Copeland Ministries* (KCM) based out of Newark, Texas. Copeland has routinely spoken on the health and wealth circuit, launched *Victory Channel* in 2015, and holds a national convention for prosperity proponents each summer in Fort Worth, Texas. Furthermore, Copeland has authored over 72 books and has facilitated a training institute known as *Believers' Academy*. The emphasis of KCM is to facilitate a two-fold partnership between believers and Kenneth Copeland (and wife, Gloria). Believers commit to sowing their financial seed into the ministry of the Copelands with the expectation of receiving the spiritual blessings that follow: healing, prosperity, and anointing.

Gloria Copeland explains the prosperity way of thinking in her own experience with privation and how they overcame it. She explains:

We focused on getting poverty out of our mouths. We began to speak words of faith (and only faith) to the mountain of debt we were facing. In 11 months the debt that had seemed so staggering a year earlier was completely paid off! We needed a car at that time, too, so we did the same thing where that was concerned. We released our faith in God's promise to supply all our needs...If you are in need of a new—or newer car—begin to put your faith muscles to work.[16]

For many, faith is a force to be wielded. And when faith is wielded rightly, according to the Copelands, it brings God's favor in tangible ways.

NEW HEIGHTS

The prosperity gospel has had many different voices throughout the last 40 years. More recently, figures like Joyce Meyer, Paula White, and T. D. Jakes have been the catalyst for the spirituality of the word of faith and prosperity movement to advance. However, it is Joel Osteen who has reached the summit of popularity among the positivity and prosperity preachers.

Osteen's brand is shot through with good-natured-awe-shucks-niceness. Pastor Osteen acts more as a spiritual coach who helps people get motivated for individual success. Osteen has even been labeled "America's Pastor," and as hard as that is to hear for some, it may be an apt description given the spiritual plight of Evangelicalism in the West. Osteen intentionally downplays sin, is light on doctrine, and is ruffled by controversial subjects.

At the center of Osteen's teaching is the power of words to shape one's reality. In his 2012 book, *I Declare: 31 Promises to Speak Over Your Life*, Osteen explains, "Our words have creative power. Whenever we speak something, either good or bad, we give life to what we are saying."[17] More succinctly, Osteen has stated in one of his most popular books, *Your Best Life Now: 7 Steps to Living at Your Full Potential,* "What you receive is directly connected to what you believe."

Osteen has become the modern repository of the seminal ideas that were at work in both Norman Vincent Peale (the power of positive thinking) and Ken Hagin (the power of one's spoken words). Osteen's platform begins with the 600,000-square-foot Lakewood Church in Houston, Texas. Lakewood Church is the biggest church in North America. Each week over 50,000 people visit to receive the optimistic and therapeutic spiritual coaching that he gives. Of course, Osteen's teaching has become nationally and internationally known through satellite radio, podcasts, books, touring, and weekly broadcasting with several companies (*Daystar, USA, TBN*).

In many respects, Osteen has become a popular punching bag of sorts in the Evangelical world. Part of this may have to do with his popularity and how much he has saturated mainstream Christianity in the West over the past twenty years. But another reason is rooted in his teaching that runs contrary to a fundamental understanding of the Christian gospel. R. Albert Mohler explains:

> Osteen has replaced the entire biblical message of Christ and what he accomplished at Golgotha. He has exchanged sacrificial atonement for self-absorption...Osteen tragically exchanges the hope of gospel centered on Christ and his accomplished work for a wishy-washy, self-centered, self-exalting message of psychotherapy. He does not proclaim the gospel but false hope. He turns the eyes of his audience away from the glory of the eternal God to a god who is a cosmic butler, waiting on our beck and call to give us health and wealth.[18]

Mohler's assessment is right. Osteen sits at the top of the prosperity movement mountain. By all optical measurements, Osteen appears to have it all. That is, all except for the Gospel of Christ. And if you do not have the Gospel, you do not have much.

LESSONS IN WOLFOLOGY

1. OUR MOTIVATION FOR GIVING SHOULD BE ROOTED IN THE ACT OF WORSHIPPING GOD WHILE ALSO RELIEVING THE BURDENS OF OTHERS.

Seed faith teaching reveals how corrupted our hearts can be with the idol of success. Instead of taking on the generosity of Christ, we make God out to be our cosmic genie, granting our wish so long as we say the right words. However, the New Testament principle in regard to giving has everything to do with proper motivation—turning this hellish idea that "we give to get" into a biblical "we get to give" perspective.

Paul explains to the Corinthian church about the pressing needs of the impoverished church in Jerusalem. He appeals to them to be bighearted in their giving, explaining to them that "God loves a cheerful giver (2 Cor 9:7)." Paul even turns to the "seed" analogy and explains that in giving:

> The point is this: whoever sows sparingly will also reap sparingly, and whoever sows bountifully will also reap bountifully…He who supplies seed to the sower and bread for food will supply and multiply your seed for sowing and increase the *harvest of your righteousness.* You will be enriched in every way to be generous in every way, which through us will *produce thanksgiving to God* (2 Cor 9:6-7, 10-11).

Paul is saying that believers should be generous in their giving, not because of what we think we might receive in material goods. Rather, giving has a sanctifying effect on the believer ("harvest of your righteousness"), and it is an act of worship ("thanksgiving to God"). What then is the reward of giving? John Stott provides a helpful answer in his commentary on Matthew 6:1-4. He writes,

> When through His gifts, the hungry are fed, the naked are clothed, the sick healed, the oppressed freed, and the lost saved…Such love which is God's own love expressed through man brings with it its own secret joys and desires no other reward.[19]

The prosperity gospel says, "We give to get," but the Christian Gospel says, "We get to give."

2. FAITH IS NOT A FORCE TO WIELD, BUT TRUST IN THE PERSON OF CHRIST.

Whenever I think of the word of faith movement I am reminded of that great religious leader of a long, long time ago—*Darth Vader*—and his ability to force-choke those who are disobedient to his commands (now that is what I call a spiritual gift). In the *Star Wars* universe, *the Force* is key to the back-and-forth battle between the Sith and the Jedi (nerd alert). In the word of faith movement, the power of positive thinking, and the power of positive confession—act as a magnet to the metal of God's blessing. However, biblical faith is centered on the essential truths of Christ.

So, faith is not a spiritual object that one can use to bend the nature of reality to their will. Instead, faith defined is a "Belief in and commitment to something or someone. Christian faith is specifically a complete trust in Christ and his work as the basis of one's relationship to God."[20] True faith brings justification to the sinner in the sight of God (Rom 3:21-26). This is not to say that some cannot be given a special gift of faith (1 Cor 12:9) that is exercised for a remarkable task for the sake of the Kingdom of God (think Esther before the king or Stephen's preaching in Acts 7). However, it does mean that Christians should rightly understand that faith is not a force to be found within our hearts and minds, but instead, it is a gift of the Holy Spirit meant to keep our spiritual sights on Christ.

3. THE PROSPERITY GOSPEL MAKES NO CATEGORY FOR SUFFERING.

Those who promote the health, wealth, and prosperity movement lack the ability to give an account for the reality of biblical suffering. Suffering is a significant theme that underscores a great deal of both the Old and New Testaments. The book of Job pulls back the divine curtain of God's theatre, and the reader discovers that it is none other than God Himself who offers Job over to Satan as a feast for suffering (Job 1:8).

If we had the power over our circumstances by the words that we say and thoughts that we think, then we suffer only because of negativity in our lives. Satan's job in all of this is to get us to think less of ourselves, while Jesus is sort of a cheerleader on the sidelines telling us "stay positive and put your best foot forward." However, Christians, just like all people in the world, experience car wrecks, cancer, violence, disease, abuse, neglect, and birth defects. There are a million different ways to suffer.

In God's paradigm, suffering is never wasted. John Piper explains, "No suffering is meaningless. None of it is wasted. The last cry of pain, leading to death, is not merely followed with glory, but rewarded with peculiar glory—a special glory prepared for the sufferer and by the suffering."[21] In other words, there is a divine purpose for our suffering, but the best the word of faith/prosperity can muster is that our suffering can end the moment we begin to speak and think optimistically.

Many parents have gone into a birthing unit with all the optimism a new child can bring. Sadly, some of them have left shattered when the child dies due to complications in the delivery ward. How does the word of faith preacher deal with that? They must theologically punt because it does not fit into any of their categories. When tragedy and suffering strike, the sufferer needs to be assured of a sovereign King (Rev 1:18-19) who not only exercises full control of their personal calamity, but He also meets them in their hardship and weeps with them there (Jn 11:35).

The tragedy of the prosperity gospel is that it makes promises that it cannot keep, all under the guise of godliness. This movement is a divine exchange program, where the word of faith teachers trade Jesus for Mammon, the truth for a lie. What does it profit anyone to gain the whole world and forfeit his soul?

Afterword: Recognizing Wolves

Beware of false prophets, who come to you in sheep's clothing but inwardly are ravenous wolves. You will recognize
them by their fruits. Are grapes gathered from thornbushes,
or figs from thistles? So, every healthy tree bears good fruit,
but the diseased tree bears bad fruit. A healthy tree cannot
bear bad fruit, nor can a diseased tree bear good fruit. Every
tree that does not bear good fruit is cut down and thrown
into the fire. Thus you will recognize them by their fruits.

—Matthew 7:15-20

A WARNING

Warnings exist for one reason—there is danger. We have alarms
on our car, in our home, and in the places we work to alert us to something potentially harmful. In Matthew 7:15-20, Jesus sounds the
alarm—*Beware of false prophets*. It is a warning to His Kingdom Citizens
about the reality of false teachers. False teachers have always been a
threat to the people of God.

The Call for Discernment

Jesus points out in Matthew 7:15 that finding out who the false
teachers are isn't always obvious. Jesus is telling us to tap into the un-
der-utilized tool called discernment. Earlier in chapter 7 (verses 5-6),
Jesus was telling His people that as they are evangelizing, they have to
use wisdom, especially as they come up against *Dogs and Hogs*. As controversial as it may seem, there are times when Christians must actually
refrain from "giving to dogs what is holy" and must hold on to "pearls"
so that the swine do not trample all over them.

We need discernment, especially dealing with issues related to false
teachers. It is possible for a false teacher to be part of the church and
to not only look like a sheep, but even serve as a shepherd. It is not
like a false teacher comes out and says, "Hi. My name is Tommy and I

plan on subverting the Holy Trinity. Do you want to do lunch at IHOP on Thursday?" If only it were that simple. No, false teachers are usually covert, not overt. Besides, wolves that are dressed like sheep can lull the church into a false sense of security that things are safe when in fact things can be quite hazardous.

Recently I was reading about *Bite Force Quotient* (BFQ). I know, I live an exciting life. However, BFQ is about what it sounds like, it measures bite-force. Now it is not surprising that a lion has a BFQ rating of 112. Nor is it any wonder that a tiger has a BFQ of 127. But think about this—a cute-cuddly-bamboo-eating panda bear has a BFQ of 160. That adorable panda could cut through your face like a chainsaw through basswood. Things are not always as they seem. Like the summer feast, when someone puts the bowl of *Cool Whip* to close to the bowl of mayonnaise—you want to be slow and discerning.

Often, false teachers use the same biblical language, but mean different things; false teachers often have a zeal, but not according to knowledge; and false teachers believe themselves to be right. Some of them even believe themselves to be shepherds to the flock. So, we need to be careful, because Jesus is telling us that false teachers are always *dressed to deceive* the people of God.

No Time for Wimpy Christianity

Another thing to notice in Matthew 7:15 is that Jesus does not pull any punches, nope, Jesus calls the false prophets "ravenous wolves (*harpax lukos*)." The words Jesus uses describe a person who is deeply cruel and bent on robbing people with a malevolent aggression. Now, there is a way for us to feel deeply and compassionately towards those who have been deceived by false teachers and false religions. Jesus wept over Jerusalem and their spiritual blindness (Lk 19:41-44). We should do the same thing. At the same time, we must be equipped with the word of God, be empowered by the Spirit of God, and have some basic understanding of the other religions and worldviews that surround us, so that we might reach people trapped in false religions.

We want to, on one hand, rescue the deceived, who are heading for the "wide gate that leads to destruction," yet on the other hand, we want to make sure false teachers do not succeed in their falsehoods. Sadly, some believe that this means that Christians must always maintain a neutral stance, or a nonchalant attitude about truth, or a call to doctrinal pacifism.

Christianity in our day has become "Peace, peace, when there is no peace (Jer 6:14)." Today is not a day for soft preaching or for soft preachers—wimpy Christianity will not survive. Pastors and churches must be willing to call out and confront those "philosophies and empty deceit" that seek to take Christians captive (Col 2:8). This is what I have tried to do in this book, to equip the reader with the basic contours of ancient and modern heresies that believers might "contend for the faith that was once and for all times been delivered to the saints (Jude v 3)." False teachers are not harmless kittens, or cute puppies—they are ravenous wolves. And they are good at hiding it too.

There should be certain weightiness pastors, elders, and church leaders feel in terms of keeping the church free from today's predators. For example, in Galatians 1:6-9, Paul emphatically pronounces a double curse upon those wolves who bring "another Gospel." Furthermore, Paul writes:

> For the time will come when people will not put up with sound doctrine. Instead, to suit their own desires, they will gather around them a great number of teachers to say what their itching ears want to hear. They will turn their ears away from the truth and turn aside to myths (2 Tim 4:3).

Since the days of the Apostles, the Church has endured heresy from without and from within. The flow of Scripture suggests that doctrinal purity will be harder as time progresses forward. Nonetheless, the watchmen of the church have a divine charter to maintain biblical orthodoxy.

HOW CAN WE RECOGNIZE FALSE TEACHERS?
Good Fruit, Bad Fruit

Jesus tells us in Matthew 7:16, "You will recognize them by their fruits." What do false teachers produce in the life of the church? Untold damages. It happens at the highest levels of upper-crust Evangelicalism to the smallest churches down backroads in Kentucky that we have never even heard of. This happens in churches when secondary doctrines are elevated above primary doctrines, or when an autocratic pastor is not held accountable by his elders and controls the church through cult of personality, or when biblical preaching is minimized and news headlines are maximized.

Jesus tells us here that we may not always see the root of the false teachers, but the fruit of the false teachers will be manifested. Jesus even gives us an illustration, He says in Matthew 7:17-18: "Are grapes gathered from thornbushes, or figs from thistles? So, every healthy tree bears good fruit, but the diseased tree bears bad fruit. A healthy tree cannot bear bad fruit, nor can a diseased tree bear good fruit."

This is easy to follow: I expect grapes from the vines, not thorn bushes; also, I expects figs from a fig tree, not thistles. Likewise, I expect ice cream from *Baskin Robbins* and not shattered glass in a cone. Jesus is simply saying that healthy, God-fearing teachers who faithfully proclaim the word of God will not sink the church with doctrinal poison, but will instead salt the church with doctrinal purity.

The Bad Fruit of False Teachers

1st Timothy 6:3-5 is Paul's case study of the bad fruit that false teachers produce. Paul writes:

> If anyone teaches a different doctrine and does not agree with the sound words of our Lord Jesus Christ and the teaching that accords with godliness, he is puffed up with conceit and understands nothing. He has an unhealthy craving for controversy and for quarrels about words, which produce envy, dissension, slander,

evil suspicions, and constant friction among people who are depraved in mind and deprived of the truth, imagining that godliness is a means of gain.

From this passage, the bad fruit of false teachers becomes discernable:

1. First, False Teachers Teach Different Doctrines (v 3a).

Good biblical teaching can take ancient words and unpack them for a modern audience (contextualizing), but it dares not adjust the Gospel of Christ for the sake of accommodation, or for the sake of modification, or capitulation. J.C. Ryle wrote, "What is the best safeguard against false doctrine? I answer in one word, 'The Bible—the Bible regularly read, regularly prayed over, regularly studied." We must go back to the old prescription of our Master: 'Diligently study the Scriptures.'"[1]

2. Second, False Teachers Reject the Sound Words of Jesus (v 3b).

False teachers are not only false because they bring some new teaching, but also because they deny the explicit teachings of the Word of God, like, rejecting the incarnation of Jesus (Docetism), or rejecting the Trinitarian nature of God (Modalism), or rejecting the doctrine of hell (Jehovah's Witnesses). In the movie *Biloxi Blues*, a corporal scolds a soldier for leaving a few bites on his tray. He looks at the soldier and says, "Take what you want, but eat what you take."[2] However, for Christians it's a little different. We are expected to eat everything on our plate of doctrine, but we don't get to choose which Christian doctrines we believe and reject. Picking and choosing works well at a cafeteria when Grandma is buying, but it never works out when you are dealing with the serious truths of Scripture. All that God wants us to believe and how He wants us to live is contained in the Word of God (2 Tim 3:16-17).

3. Third, False Teachers are Consumed with Self-Interest (v 4a).

The Scriptures say that pride goes before a fall (Pro 16:18). It also reveals an enormous character flaw in the life of a false teacher—egotism. Steven Cole is a preacher who has helped a whole generation of pastors through his sermons that have been proliferated through many internet outlets; for good reason too, Cole is a solid expositor, plain spoken, and an enjoyable to read, a J.C. Ryle for my generation (maybe, let us keep Steve humble). In his exposition of Matthew 6:3-5, he said, "False teaching starts with man, centers on man, and builds up man."[3] Scripture identifies "conceit" as a specific tendency in the life of those who seek to pull the church away from the doctrines of Jesus.

4. Fourth, False Teachers Thrive on Dividing the Body of Christ (v 4b).

False teachers cause division. In 2020, I have seen more division in Evangelicalism in one year than all my years as a Christian combined. Christendom is divided in the United States today over issues like racial identitarianism, social issues, and "Wokeness." Some of the division is necessary. As Martin Luther famously said, "Peace if possible, but the truth at all costs." However, there is a kind of person who courts controversy at every angle. They tend to see themselves as a hammer. And when that happens, they also tend to see everyone and everything as a nail. This causes division. Schisms have always been ranked right alongside apostasy and heresy, usually because the three go together, an unholy trinity of sorts.

5. Fifth, False Teachers are Motivated by Power, Materials, or Wealth (v 5).

Some teachers are motivated to be in ministry not for the glory of God and the good of His name, but what they can personally gain. Costi Hinn, nephew to the prosperity teacher Benny Hinn, was radically changed by the Gospel of Christ in his college years. In 2019, Costi wrote a book entitled, *God, Greed, and the Prosperity Gospel: How Truth Overwhelms a Life Built on Lies.*

It is a candid portrayal of what *the best life and blessed life* look like from an insider's perspective of the prosperity movement. Hinn expressed, "The prosperity gospel pays amazingly well, and so do shady business deals that go on in the background, and we had the toys to prove it."[4] Prosperity teachers are not the only ones affected by this; all false teachers are motivated into "ministry" for the wrong reasons.

CONCLUSION

In the safety of our orthodox fortresses (church buildings, Sunday schools, and home groups), we sometimes forget that through the remainder of each week that we can easily drift from truth (Heb 2:1). That is why the fellowship of the church, godly leadership, and daily discipleship is so important to our walk with Christ. There are many competing voices for our eyes and ears, and our hearts and minds. The late R.C. Sproul stated, "We have to open our ears to the teaching of Jesus and close our ears to the teaching of the culture, which has everything upside down."[5]

Appendix A
The Bethel Movement (NAR)

Started in the mid-1950s, Bethel Church (Redding, California) eventually broke away from the Assemblies of God denomination in 2006. Under the pastoral leadership of Bill and Beni Johnson, Bethel Church blossomed into a megachurch of 11,000 members since the couple took the helm of leadership in 1996.[1] Grown out of the intertwined movements of both the *Latter Rain* movement as well as Charismatic-Pentecostal renewalism, Bethel is at the center of *The New Apostolic Reformation* (NAR).[2] The NAR is a modern restoration movement that deems itself to be a return to days of the miracles of the early church and restore the "lost office" of the Apostles.[3]

Driven by a postmillennialish eschatological impulse—the NAR can be described as the evolution of the faith healing spectrum that was at work in earlier iterations of the Word of Faith movement (Chapter 7). Though not a formal denomination, the NAR has received "formal recognition...by sociologists of religion, church historians and scholars."[4] The leading proliferator of the NAR movement has been Bethel church and the teachings of Bill Johnson.

Courting controversy, Johnson's *Kingdom Now* theology is an outworking of his belief in the restoration of true apostolic Christianity. Kingdom Now theology is defined as a:

> Visible dominance of God's kingdom on earth, and to conquer every area of human existence, leading people into submission to Christ...The definition of this theology can be seen in its purpose. In its eschatology, this theology is led by the assumption that God's kingdom can come to earth through human help, i.e. Christ shall not return until the church takes the power from Satan and his followers, thus establishing dominion on earth.[5]

Johnson believes that it is up to NAR/Kingdom Now followers to snag-hook heaven and reel it down to earth through performing "signs and wonders." Hermeneutically, the NAR advocates an absolutizing of the book of Acts as a prescription of the kind of dominion that the church should exercise today in the power of the Holy Spirit.[6]

With some regularity, gold-dusting (a practice whereby gold glitter pours down from the rafters) and feathers (an angelic fly-by?) make appearances during Bethel worship—supposedly a sign from God. However, these parlor tricks have been debunked both in and out of charismatic circles.[7] One could forgive the charlatan nature of these gestures in the same way parents entertain their children with fairy tales, but there has been one exploitive trick that is as horrific as it is tragic.

In December of 2019, a young two-year old girl named Olive Heiligenthal passed away suddenly. Kalley Heiligenthal, Olive's mother, a member of Bethel Church and part of the music ministry, requested that Bethel Church engage in prayer to raise Olive from the dead.[8] As the reader might suspect, they were unsuccessful. Some may say that it is commendable for a church to have such a firm belief in the supernatural that they committed themselves to pray for God to raise the dead. After all, Bethel has a ministry called *The Dead Raising Team* (deadraisingteam.com) that has boasted of raising multiple people from the dead.[9] The Dead Raising Team flows out of the *Bethel Supernatural School of Ministry* (sort of like *Hogwarts* with Jesus banners everywhere, minus the golden snitch).

Bethel Church and the NAR walk in dangerous steps of Smith Wigglesworth and those like him, even participating in the necromancy of "grave soaking" (the practice of trying to absorb the anointing of the deceased)."[10] Not only conning people in the name of Jesus, but also exploiting people who are suffering by giving them hope in miracles that God never promised to them.

Now, can God still perform miracles? Yes. No Bible-believing Christian doubts that God does whatever He pleases (Ps 115:3); however, there is good reason to believe that the signs and wonders that occurred in the book of the Acts were meant to attest to authenticity and authority of the Apostles (2 Cor 12:11-13; Acts 4:30; 5:1-10, 12-16; 14:3), not meant to be taken as a normative experience.

Based purely on Johnson's theology there are glaring instances of biblical incoherency, especially as this relates to the person of Jesus Christ. Johnson states,

> Jesus reflected perfect theology both in what He showed us of the Father and what He showed us about carrying out the Father's will. Jesus emptied Himself of divinity and became man. While He is eternally God, He chose to live within the restrictions of a man who had no sin and was empowered by the Holy Spirit.[11]

Here Johnson advocates for *Kenosis Theory* (*Kenosis* means "to empty" cf. Phil 2:5-8). Kenosis Theory is a deficient Christology that proposes that Jesus divested Himself of His deity during the time of His earthly ministry (it sort of runs in a trajectory similar to that of the Adoptionists). In this view, Jesus is perfect man by virtue of the Spirit's power. Let us take some time to examine the major problems with Kenosis theory:

1. First, Jesus is Eternally God (Jn 1:1-2; Col 1:15). There was never a time when Jesus was not God (see the *Chalcedonic Definition* at the end of Chapter 3).

2. Second, as an ontological axiom, God can never cease from being God. Think about it. Creation would dissolve into the horror of nihilism if the One who held creation together set aside His capacity to do so (Col 1:16).

3. Third, the idea that Jesus could empty Himself of His deity would collapse the unity of the Trinity into an unbiblical version of binitarianism.

4. Fourth, God's immutability forbids the notion that Christ's deity could be turned off (Num 23:19; Mal 3:6).

5. Fifth, if Jesus's deity were truly laid aside it would prove that Jesus's death was impotent to save sinners from the wrath of God.[12]

Bethel Church has become popular not only through the local ministry of the church in Redding, but also through the successful writing ministry of Bill Johnson. A couple of Johnson's most popular books are *When Heaven Invades Earth* (2009) and *The Way of Life: Experiencing the Culture of Heaven on Earth* (2018). Likewise, the popularity of the music that has come out of Bethel has received an incredible audience. The music group *Jesus Culture* was born out of Bethel in 1999. Jesus Culture has had numerous hits like *Your Love Never Fails, How He Loves Us,* and *Break Every Chain.* Furthermore, *Bethel Music* has become its own brand and produced mega-evangelical hits like *We Will Not be Shaken* and *Raise a Hallelujah.* Regardless of what one thinks about the theology of Bethel—they have become titans in the media world of mainstream Evangelicalism.

Should Christians sing Bethel Music? Well, would you sing explicitly Mormon hymns (i.e. *We Thank Thee, O God, for a Prophet*)? How you answer the second question should help you answer the first, because the Bethel movement teaches a faulty view of Christ just as the Church of Jesus Christ of Latter-day Saints. The esoteric and Occultic nature of Bethel's mystical practices such as "grave soaking" and their attempts at raising the dead are alarming in and of themselves, but purely on the Christological level the movement should be branded as heterodox institution. Bethel may be accepted by much of the Evangelical world both in the United States and globally, but since when has popularity ever been the measure of biblical faithfulness (2 Tim 4:3; Jn 6:60-66)?

Appendix B
Baptismal Regeneration

For over 500 years, Protestants have proclaimed that salvation is wholly owning to the gracious mercy of the sovereign God (*Sola Gratia*). In the Canons of Dort (1618-1619), the authors expressed what the Scriptures make plain, which is:

> Faith is a gift of God, not in the sense that it is offered by God for people to choose, but that it is in actual fact bestowed on them, breathed and infused into them. Nor is it a gift in the sense that God bestows only the potential to believe, but then awaits assent—the act of believing—by human choice; rather, it is a gift in the sense that God who works both willing and acting and, indeed, works all things in all people and produces in them both the will to believe and the belief itself.[1]

Salvation is only by the grace of God (Eph 2:8-9). However, there have been some movements throughout the history of the church that have made baptism a central feature of salvation (i.e. *Baptismal Regeneration*).

Let us take a moment and define baptism. Baptism comes from the Greek word *baptizo*, which means to dip or immerse into water. Baptism is an ancient rite that Jesus ordained in the Gospels for all His disciples to obey throughout the church age (Mt 28:19-20). However, over the past 2,000 years the church debated over baptism extensively:

- *Who should be baptized?* Infants of believers, or only adults who have professed faith in Christ?

- *What does baptism signify?* Is baptism only a sign, or is it a seal? Is it an ordinance, or a sacrament, or both?

- *What mode of baptism should the church institute?* Should baptism be done by sprinkling, pouring, or by immersion?

- *What does baptism do?* Is it just an initiation, or an instrument? Is it *a* means of grace, or is it *the* means of grace?

The Christian tradition you come out of largely shapes your basic understanding of baptism, and among born-again believers there can be gracious debate about the nature of baptism, so long as nobody makes baptism essential for salvation.

We should hold baptism in high regard while at the same time dispelling the misinterpretations of Scripture regarding baptism. Baptism is the initiatory event of the believer as they join the body of Christ, the church (Mt 28:19-20; Acts 2:38). I remember my own baptismal waters (a long, long time ago in a baptistry far, far away) and what it represented then and what it still means to me now. I remember the Sunday I baptized my own son, Piper, into the church. It was an incredible day that we celebrated as a family and as a church body. We were celebrating the outward sign of what God had already performed inwardly in the heart.

In baptism, we get to see the tangible drama of the Gospel played out in the act of baptism: down into the waters the old life has died, up from the waters we see resurrection, and walking out from the water we see the newness of life. Isn't it something? God has given us this outward sign (Rom 6:3-5), not only for those who are going through ritual, but also for the entire body of Christ to see—again and again—every time the Gospel saves a sinner.

Sadly, some movements have placed baptism at the center of their salvation. In their mind, they believe they elevate the significance of baptism, but the truth is they undermine the Gospel of Christ that saves which makes their baptism nothing more than a public bath. Below you will find a snapshot of the movements that, to varying degrees, teach baptismal regeneration/justification.

1. Roman Catholicism. According to the Roman Catholic Catechism, baptism is a "central rite" that "brings about the birth of water and Spirit without which no one 'can enter the kingdom of God.'"[2] Furthermore, the Roman Catholic Catechism says, "By Baptism all sins are forgiven, original sin and all personal sins, as well as punishment for sins."[3] In Roman Catholicism, baptism is not only one of seven sacraments of the church, but it is also essential to the salvation of the believer.

2. Greek Orthodoxy. The *Greek Orthodox Diocese of America* explains "By Baptism, the Church holds that all optional and original sins are cleansed by the Grace of God. The Chrismation [consecration with oil] of a newly baptized person is the confirmation of his faith which is 'the seal of the gift of the Holy Ghost.'"[4] The two-fold act of baptism and chrism, combined, are crucial to salvation.

3. The Churches of Christ. According to a Church of Christ website, a person is saved in the following manner:

> Though God's part is the big part, man's part is also necessary if man is to reach heaven. Man must comply with the conditions of pardon which the Lord has announced. Man's part can clearly set forth in the following steps: [1] Hear the Gospel; [2] Believe; [3] Repent of past sins [4] Confess Jesus as Lord; [5] Be baptized for the remission of sins; [6] Live a Christian life.[5]

In fairness to the Churches of Christ, their churches are autonomous and it is likely that their beliefs would range and vary from congregation to congregation. Likewise, there is much in the statement above that is agreeable and in accord with Scripture; no Christian would disagree with the essentials: hear the Gospel, believe the Gospel, repent of sin, and confess Christ as Lord. The problem is to say that "Man must comply with the conditions of pardon which the Lord has announced" and then unbiblically asserting that baptism must be performed.

4. The International Churches of Christ. The International Church of Christ (ICOC) was borne out of the Church of Christ movement during the late 1970s through the efforts of founder, Kip McKean.[6] Like most Restoration movements, the ICOC's creed is, "No creed but Christ, no book but the Bible."[7] The ICOC is a global association of churches that emphasize local church autonomy and a decentralized ecclesiastical authority. That is why it is no wonder when one goes hunting for the uniform body of beliefs that it may be difficult to find. Nonetheless, when you do a search for ICOC churches you will find basically what you find in the Church of Christ—the mixture of God's grace plus man's baptism. [8]

5. United Pentecostal Church International. According to the official United Pentecostal Church International's 2017 manual,

> The basic and fundamental doctrine of this organization shall be the Bible standard of full salvation, which is repentance, baptism in water by immersion in the name of the Lord Jesus Christ for the remission of sins, and the baptism of the Holy Ghost with the initial sign of speaking with other tongues as the Spirit gives utterance.[9]

Two Criticisms of Baptismal Regeneration

1. Baptismal Regeneration Rejects Salvation by Grace Alone. Scripture teaches that salvation is by grace alone (Ez 37:5-6; Rom 9:15-16; Eph 2:8-9), through faith alone (Rom 1:16-17; 3:21-26; 4:1-6), in Christ alone (Jn 3:16; 14:6). Scripture places an emphasis upon the initiatory actions of God to bestow salvation upon the unworthy sinner (Rom 5:6; 6:23). Baptism, as important as it is, is insufficient to save. Anyone who believes that salvation depends on baptism has grossly distorted the biblical concept of God's grace.

2. Baptismal Regeneration Arises from Absolutizing Baptism Texts. A classic example of this is Acts 2:38, which reads, "Repent and be baptized every one of you in the name of Jesus Christ for the forgiveness of your sins." On the surface, it appears that repentance and baptism are the means of obtaining forgiveness. There are other texts like this as well (Mk 16:16; Jn 3:5; Acts 22:16), but they fail to harmonize baptismal-texts with texts that emphasize salvation by grace (Rom 5:1-2; Rom 6:23; Ti 3:5).

Proper biblical exegesis, that accounts for the context, syntax, and the rule of faith (*regula fidei*), would interpret Acts 2:38 by arguing that:

- Salvation is not accomplished by what occurs in Acts 2:38 through baptism. Instead, we begin to see the regenerative power of the Holy Spirit in the preceding context of Acts 2:37 (i.e. the hearers of Peter's Gospel message were "cut to the heart") compare this language with Ezekiel 36:25 and John 3:1-9. The Holy Spirit is the

One who wrought salvation. Likewise, those who are interpreting Lukan soteriology in Acts should read it through the lens of Acts 13:38, "and as many as were appointed to eternal life believed." Regeneration will lead a sinner to repent and then be baptized. Ultimately, God's sovereign grace and electing purposes are what count in the saving of sinners (Eph 1:4-5).

- Here is an expanded technical explanation concerning the syntax by Luther McIntire, he says "Acts 2:38 in fact demonstrates perfect concord between pronoun and verb in the case of both 'repent' and 'be baptized' The passage can be diagrammed as follows.

    >Repent [second person plural]
        *be baptized [third person singular]
        *each [third person singular] of you
    >for the remission of your [second person plural] sins.

    This structure illustrates that the command to be baptized is parenthetical and is not syntactically connected to remission of sins. When Peter commanded the people to repent, he was speaking to the crowd. Then the command to be baptized was directed to each individual. In the 'remission of your sins' phrase, Peter again directed his words to the crowd collectively."[10]

- Proponents of baptismal regeneration render "for" (*eis*) in Acts 2:38, as the means of obtaining "forgiveness." What Luke is conveying in Acts 2:38 is not to be "baptized" *to gain* "the forgiveness of your sins," but rather to be baptized *into* Jesus's name. For example, 1st Corinthians 10:2 says that Israelites were "baptized into [*eis*] Moses." Being baptized into Moses was one of the ways Israel identified with Moses; and now, when followers of Christ believe, they also are baptized into Jesus that they may identify with Him.[11]

- Consider Acts 10:44-48 Those verses describe salvation in the following manner: 1) Peter is preaching to Cornelius and other Gentiles (proclamation); 2) the Holy Spirit falls (regeneration); 3) the Gentiles speak in tongues (manifestation); and finally, 4) Peter commands the Gentile believers to be "baptized in the name of Jesus Christ (initiation)." My point is simple: Acts 10:44-48 clearly shows that regeneration (salvation) occurs prior to initiation (baptism) and not the other way around.

Appendix C
Christians and Secret Societies

What exactly is a *Secret Society?* Philip Gardiner defines a secret society this way:

> It is simply a group of individuals, basing their origin in the mists of time or in the celestial and solar dance of the cyclic universe, who come together to affect change. Sometimes they are successful, sometimes they are not, but in most cases, they affect some kind of change in society at large.[1]

Secret societies are not necessarily a secret to society, but they are secretive in the way that the organization acts. Secret societies have existed since the days of Pythagoras (570 B.C.-470 B.C.).[2] Some secret societies have ravaged culture at times, movements like the *Ku Klux Klan* and the *Nazis*. Other secret societies argue that their existence is to meet a real need in their communities. Consider *The Knights of Pythias* as an example—they proclaim that the way to happiness is "through service to mankind."[3]

Other well-known secret societies have allegedly influenced nations and states, as well as governing the building of societies. Movements like Yale's *Skull and Bones* has had members that have been Presidents of the United States (William H. Taft, both George H.W. Bush and George W. Bush), industrial leaders (Howell Cheney and Eddie Lampert), and cultural influencers (William F. Buckley and Robert Kagan). Likewise, the Freemasons had members that are some of the most towering figures of history: George Washington, Ben Franklin, and Winston Churchill. Even the Southern Baptist Theological Seminary had a secret society (*Dodeka*) at one point in time, for a group of Baptist elites.[4]

Of course, there is the whole Greek Fraternity/Sorority structure that is part-and-parcel of life on college campuses all over the United States. Some fraternities date all the way back to the founding of the

United States of America (*Phi Beta Kappa*, 1775). Many of these groups have a specific charter; for example, the sorority *Kappa Delta Phi* began in 1977 with the goal,

> To develop the highest philanthropic ideals possible within each chapter and individual sister. Providing service to others is the cornerstone on which this Sorority was built. We continue to build on that through various service projects and activities for both the campus and surrounding communities.[5]

On the surface, the Greek fraternity system seems not only harmless, but even helpful—sort of a social club with the goal relieving societal problems. However, it has been well documented that physical, emotional, and sexual abuse has occurred during some of the hazing-rituals (often called *Hell Week*) that accompany these longstanding institutions.[6]

So, what should be the Christians' response to secret societies and fraternities & sororities? In the first place, it should be obvious to born-again Christians that hate groups like the *KKK* and the various Neo-Nazi groups that are motivated by racial superiority are explicitly sinful (Rom 2:11; Gal 3:28). Any Christian found participating in a group like this should be called to repentance and if necessary be excommunicated by the church (Mt 18:15-20). Secondly, I would be wary about a believer taking part in non-Christian rituals and the explicit syncretism of such a gathering. Consider the following statement about Freemasonry,

> Freemasonry is not a religion, nor is it a substitute for religion. It requires of its members a belief in God as part of the obligation of every responsible adult, but advocates no sectarian faith or practice. Masonic ceremonies include prayers, both traditional and extempore, to reaffirm each individual's dependence on God and to seek divine guidance. Freemasonry is open to men of any faith, but religion may not be discussed at Masonic meetings...Masonry primarily uses the appellation, "Grand Architect of the Universe," and other non-sectarian titles, to address the Deity. In this way, persons of different faiths may join together in prayer, concentrating on God, rather than differences among themselves.[7]

Christians should not be yoked to non-Christians or those of different faiths, especially in a sphere of worship, for three reasons: first, it demeans the exclusivity of Christianity with the one true faith ("What accord has Christ with Belial," 2 Cor 6:15); second, it clouds the object of the Christian's true worship which is not an opaque, generic, god-in-a-box, but the One true Almighty—revealed in glorious Trinity—Father, Son, and Holy Ghost (1 Cor 8:6; 2 Cor 3:17; 13:14; Mt 3:16-17); third, the Christian who is participating in such an event might be suggesting to non-Christians present that a relationship with Jesus is not necessary to be in a right relationship to God (Jn 14:6).

Another reason for Christians to reject secret societies is the pledged secrecy of such participation. Jesus tells us, "Whatever you have said in the dark shall be heard in the light, and what you have whispered in private rooms shall be proclaimed on the housetops (Lk 12:3)." He also says, "You are the light of the world. A city set on a hill cannot be hidden. Nor do people light a lamp and put it under a basket, but on a stand, and it gives light to all in the house. In the same way, let your light shine before others (Mt 5:14-16)." Secret meetings, secret rituals, and secret societies run contrary to the basic precept Jesus sets forth—*Christians are not tucked away in darkness, but openly shine light.*

Finally, and maybe most importantly, the problem with Christians participating in secret social clubs is that it runs the risk of dividing a believer's allegiance to Christ and the local church (Lk 16:13). One could envision a scenario where one's pledge of allegiance at the local lodge could run into conflict with their responsibility to the body of Christ. Likewise, a young man or a young woman could go off to college and look to a sorority or a fraternity for a new sense of belonging and identity, when in fact they should belong to a local church and find their identity in Jesus (2 Cor 5:17b).

Most Christians who are involved in sororities, fraternities, or other secret clubs are not overtly trying to subvert the local church nor undermine their Gospel witness. Like a lot of things, it may well be that there is a high degree of ignorance and pressure to conform. All the same, I would not encourage any believer in the Lord Jesus Christ to unite themselves to any hidden society/club, regardless of how positive the group's charter and no matter how harmless it all seems. Christians do not belong to the darkness—they belong to the light (Col 2:13).

Notes

INTRODUCTION

[1] L. David Mech, *The Wolf: The Ecology and Behavior of an Endangered Species*. New York: Doubleday, 1970.

CHAPTER 1: ARIANISM

[1] A.W. Pink, *The Attributes of God* (Seattle: Amazon Digital Services, 2010, Kindle Edition), 38.

[2] Mark Jones, *God Is: A Devotional Guide to the Attributes of God* (Wheaton: Crossway, 2017), 228.

[3] Edward Hardly, ed.,*Christology of the Later Fathers*, ed. (Louisville, KY: Westminster John Knox, 1954), 332-333.

[4] Caesar Morgan, *An Investigation of the Trinity of Plato and Philo Judaeus, and of the Effects which an Attachment to Their Writings Had Upon the Principles and Reasonings of the Fathers of the Christian Church* (London: Cambridge University Press, 1853), 143.

[5] *NPNF 2.4 Nicene and Post-Nicene Fathers of the Christian Church*. Edited by Philip Schaff 1886. 28 vols. Repr. (Grand Rapids, MI: Christian Classic Ethereal Library, 2005).

[6] Carlos Galvao-Sobrinho, "Embodied Theologies: Christian Identity and Violence in Alexandria in the Early Arian Controversy," in *Violence in Late Antiquity: Perception and Practice* ed., Henry Drake (Burlington, VT: Ashgate, 2003), 321.

[7] Dan Graves, "Article 11: In Hoc Signes Vinces," https://christianhistoryinstitute.org/in-context/article/constantines-cross

[8] Tobby E. Smith, "The Blessings of Battle: How Theological Struggle Between Arianism and Athanasius the Boundaries of Christological Orthodoxy," a paper presented for Early Christian History, Midwestern Baptist Theological Seminary, July 27, 2018.

[9] Alister McGrath, *Christian History: An Introduction*, 3rd edition (Oxford, John Wiley and Sons, 2015), 86.

[10] John Wayland Coakley and Andrea Sterk, eds., *Readings in World Christian History: Early Christianity to 1453* (Maryknoll: Orbis, 2004), 97.

[11] Karl Joseph Von Helefe explains in his work *To the Close of Nicaea, A.D. 325: From the Original Documents*, Second edition (Edinburgh: T & T Clark, 1894), 286, that "At Nicaea orthodox bishops formed, along with Athanasius and his friends, the right; Arius... the left; whilst the left centre was occupied by the Eusebians, and right centre Eusebius of Caesarea."

[12] *Saint Nicholas Orthodox Church,* "St. Nicholas the Wonder Worker—Our Patron Saint," https://www.stnicholasorthodox.org/patronsaint.

[13] Wayne Grudem, *Systematic Theology* (Grand Rapids: Zondervan, 1994), 193.

[14] R.P.C. Hanson, *The Search for the Christian Doctrine of God: The Arian Controversy 318-381* (New York: T & T Clark, 2005), 163.

[15] St. Jerome, *The Dialogue with the Luciferians* (Seattle: CreateSpace), 20.

16 Smith, "The Blessings of Battle," 19-20.

17 David Allen Clark, Donald Koch, and Mark Harris, "A Strange Way to Save the World," Universal Music Publishing, 1993. Accessed Nov 20, 2020.

18 Modified from "holy Catholic" to "holy Christian" to mitigate the confusion that comes with the language of the universal Church (Catholic) that is largely misunderstood in Protestant circles.

CHAPTER 2: GNOSTICISM

1 Everett Ferguson, *Church History, Volume One:* From Christ to Pre-Reformation: The Rise and Growth of the Church in Its Cultural, Intellectual, and Political Context (Grand Rapids: Zondervan, 2005, Kindle Edition), Kindle Location 1721-1723.

2 Greg Allison, *The Baker Compact Dictionary of Theological Terms* (Grand Rapids: Baker, 2016), 89.

3 Rachel L. Wagner, "Wake Up! Gnosticism and Buddhism in the Matrix," *Journal of Religion and Film* 5 (2016): 4.

4 Eusebius, *The History of the Church from Christ to Constantine*, translated by G.A. Williamson (New York: Penguin, 1989), 144.

5 Justin Holcomb, *Know the Heretics* (Grand Rapids: Zondervan, 2014), 34.

6 Mitch Horowitz, *Occult America: White House Seances, Ouija Circles, Masons, and the Secret Mystics of our Nation* (New York: Bantam, 2009), 49.

7 Hugh Urban, "The Knowing of Knowing: Neo-Gnosticism from the OTO to Scientology," *Gnosis: Journal of Gnostic Studies* 4 (2019): 99-102.

8 John Pennachio, "Gnostic Inner Illumination and Carl Jung's Individuation," *Journal of Religion and Health* 31 (1992): 238.

9 Giles Quispel, "Meetings with Jung," in *Edges of Experience: Memory and Emergence: Proceedings of the Sixteenth International Congress for Analytical Psychology*, ed. L. Cowan (Einsiedeln: Daimon, 2006), 145-52.

10 Hans Jonas, "Gnosticism and Modern Nihilism," *Social Research* 19 (1952): 433.

11 Shelby Grad and David Colker, "Nancy Regan Turned to astrology in White House to protect her husband," *The Los Angelos Times*, March 6, 2016.

12 Larry and Andy Wachowski, *The Matrix*, transcripted by Tim Staley. 1999.

13 *The Gnostic Library: Nag Hammadi codices II, 1: III, 1; and VI; Nag Hammadi codex II, 2-7; Nag Hammadi codices III, 2 and IV, 2.* (Claremont: Institute for Antiquity and Christianity, 2000), 2009.

14 Eckhart Tolle, *A New Earth: Awakening to Your Life's Purpose* (New York: Penguin, 2016), 6.

15 Ibid., 7.

16 Deepak Chopra, *The Seven Spiritual Laws of Success: A Practical Guide to the Fulfillment of Your Dreams* (New York: Amber-Allen Publishing, 1993), *v.*

17 R.C. Sproul, *The Holiness of God* (Carol Stream: Tyndale, 1998), 108.

[18] Douglas Groothius, "The Gnostic Jesus," https://www.equip.org /article/the-gnostic-jesus.

[19] *The Heidelberg Catechism* (Grand Rapids: Christian Reformed Church, 1975), Q&A 15.

CHAPTER 3: SABELLIANISM/MODALISM

[1] Alister McGrath, *Heresy: A History of Defending the Truth* (New York: Harper Collins, 2009), 106.

[2] J.H. Kurtz, *Church History, volumes 1-3* (London: Butler & Tanner, e-book), 33.3.

[3] Millard Erickson, *Christian Theology* (Grand Rapids: Baker, 1986), 333.

[4] Dragos Andrei Giulea, "Antioch 268 and Its Legacy in the Fourth Century Theological Debates," *Harvard Theological Review* 111 (2018): 192.

[5] Millard Erickson, *Concise Dictionary of Theological Terms* (Wheaton: Crossway, 2001), 126.

[6] Bryan Litfin, "Tertullian on the Trinity," *Perichoresis* 17 (2019): 89.

[7] Joseph Kelly, *History and Heresy: How Historical Forces Can Create Doctrinal Conflicts* (Collegeville: Liturgical Press, 2012), 43.

[8] Tertullian, *Against Praxeas: In which he defends, in all essential points, the doctrine of the Holy Trinity* (Seattle: Aeterna Press, 2010), Kindle Location 19.

[9] Belgic Confession of Faith (1561), article 9. https://www.crcna.org /welcome/beliefs/confessions/belgic-confession.

[10] Justin Holcomb, *Know the Heretics* (Grand Rapids: Zondervan, 2014), 78.

[11] Edward Dalcour, *A Definitive Look at Oneness Theology: In the Light of Biblical Trinitarianism,* 4th edition, adapted from PhD Thesis: "An Evaluation of 'Oneness Theology' in the Light of the Biblical Emphasis of Trinitarianism," (Potchefstroom: North-West University, 2016), 142.

[12] Julia Corbett Hemeyer, *Religion in American,* 6th edition (New York: Routledge, 2016), 248.

[13] Dalcour, *A Definitive Look,"* 13.

[14] "About UPCI," https://www.upci.org/about/about-the-upci.

[15] Richard Gimpel, "The Oneness Theology of the United Pentecostal Church International" (M.A. Thesis, Reformed Theological Seminary, 1999), 15-17.

[16] Ibid.

[17] Ibid.

[18] Greg Boyd, *Oneness Pentecostals and the Trinity: A World-wide Movement Assessed by a former Oneness Pentecostal* (Grand Rapids: Baker, 1992), 26.

[19] Carl Trueman, "Problematic Analogies and Prayerful Adoration," https://www.ligonier.org/learn/articles/problematic-analogies-and-prayerful-adoration/.

[20] Philip Schaff, *Creeds of Christendom, Volumes 1-3: A History and Critical Notes* (New York, NY: Harper & Brothers, 1919; 2016 Delmarva Publications Kindle Edition), Kindle Location 33790-33942.

[21] R.C. Sproul, *Who is the Holy Spirit?* (North Manakato: Reformation Trust, 2012), 10.

22 I have substituted the word Christian for Catholic for the sake of making a simple distinction between Roman Catholicism and Universal Christianity.

CHAPTER 4: MORMONISM

1 The Church of Jesus Christ of Latter-day Saints. *The History of the Church, volume 1* (Salt Lake City: The Church of Jesus Christ of Latter-day Saints, 1948), 1:106.

2 The Church of Jesus Christ of Latter-day Saints, "Restoration of the Gospel" in *True to the Faith* (Salt Lake City: The Church of Jesus Christ of Latter-day Saints, 2004), 13-14.

3 Harold Bloom, *The American Religion* (New York: Chu Hartley, 2013), Kindle Location 1128.

4 The Church of Jesus Christ of Latter-day Saints. *The Pearl of Great Price: Joseph Smith History—1* (Salt Lake City: The Church of Jesus Christ of Latter-day Saints, 2013): 1:12-20.

5 Susan Stansfield Wolverton, *Having Visions: The Book of Mormon Translated and Exposed in Plain Language* (New York: Algora, 2014).

6 "Race and Priesthood," *Gospel Topics Essays* (2016) The Church of Jesus Christ of Latter-day Saints. https://www.churchofjesuschrist.org/manual/gospel-topics-essays/race-and-the-priesthood?lang=eng.

7 The Church of Jesus Christ of Latter-day Saints. *The Book of Mormon* (Salt Lake City: The Church of Jesus Christ of Latter-day Saints, 2013), 3 Nephi 11:8-10.

8 "The Witnesses of the Book of Mormon," https://www.churchofjesus christ.org /bc/content/shared/content/images/gospel-library/manual/32506/32506_000_057_03-witnesses.pdf.

9 *The Book of Mormon,* "The Testimony of the Three Witnesses," 5.

10 *The Book of Mormon,* "The Testimony of the Eight Witnesses," 6.

11 James Lancaster, "The Translation of the Book of Mormon" in *The Word of God*, ed. Dan Vogel (Salt Lake City: Signature, 1990), 98-99.

12 There are two works that I commend to you on the subject. The first is D. Michael Quinn's *Early Mormonism and the Magic Worldview* (Salt Lake City: Signature, 1998) and David Horowitz's *Occult in America: White House Seances, Ouija Circles, Masons, and the Secret Mystic History of Our Nation* (New York: Bantam, 2010).

13 Steven Harper, "The Probation of a Teenage Seer: Joseph Smith's Early Experience with Moroni" in *The Coming Forth of the Book of Mormon: The 44th Annual BYU Sidney B. Sperry Symposium*, eds. Dennis Largey, Andrew Hedges, John Hilton, and Kerry Hull (Salt Lake City: Deseret 2015), 42.

14 Joe Carter, "9 Things You Should Know About the Bethel Church Movement," https://www.thegospelcoalition.org/article/9-things-you-should-know-about-the-bethel-church-movement/.

15 "The Church of Jesus Christ of Latter-day Saints. *The History of the Church, volume 4* (Salt Lake City: The Church of Jesus Christ of Latter-day Saints, 1948), 4:461.

16 See Jerald and Sandra Tanner's *3,913 Changes to the Book of Mormon* (Salt Lake City: Utah Lighthouse Ministry, 1996).

17 James Lancaster, "The Translation of the Book of Mormon" in *The Word of God*, ed. Dan Vogel (Salt Lake City: Signature, 1990), 98-99.

18 "Facts and Statistics," *The Church of Jesus Christ of Latter-day Saints. https://newsroom.churchofjesuschrist.org/facts-and-statistics.*

19 The Church of Jesus Christ of Latter-day Saints. *The History of the Church, volume 6* (Salt Lake City: The Church of Jesus Christ of Latter-day Saints, 1948): 305.

20 "Is President Lorenzo Snow's oft-repeated statement—"As man now is, God once was; as God now is, man may be"—accepted as official doctrine by the Church?" *Ensign,* February 1982. https://www.churchofjesuschrist.org/study/ensign/1982/02/ i-have-a-question/is-president-snows-statement-as-man-now-is-god-once-was-as-god-now-is-man-may-be-accepted-as-official-doctrine?lang=eng.

21 Richard Mouw, "Mormons Approaching Orthodoxy," *First Things* May 2016, https://www.firstthings.com/article/2016/05/mormons-approaching-orthodoxy.

22 "The Articles of Faith of the Church of Jesus Christ of Latter-day Saints," https://www.churchofjesuschrist.org/study/Scriptures/pgp/a-of-f/1?lang=eng.

23 *The Church of Jesus Christ of Latter-day Saints*, "Are you saved by Grace or Works?" *Ensign* March (2005): 38.

24 "Southern Baptists vs. The Mormons," Neil Young, http://www.slate.com/articles/life/faithbased/2007/12/southern_baptists_vs_the_mormons.html.

25 Trevin Wax, *Counterfeit Gospels: Rediscovering the Good News in a World of False Hope* (Chicago: Moody Press, 2011), 13.

CHAPTER 5: JEHOVAH'S WITNESSES

1 Simran Khuran, "Quotes by Mark Twain on Religion," https://www .thoughtco.com/religion-quotes-by-mark-twain-2832666.

2 Quran, *An-Nisa* verse 115.

3 The Church of Jesus Christ of Latter-day Saints. *The Book of Mormon* (Salt Lake City: The Church of Jesus Christ of Latter-day Saints, 2013), 3 Nephi 11:8-10.

4 The Watchtower Bible and Tract Society, "You Can Live Forever On the Earth—But How," *The Watchtower* Feb (1983): 12-15.

5 The Watchtower Bible and Tract Society, *You Can Live Forever in Paradise on the Earth* (Brooklyn: The Watchtower Bible and Tract Society, 1982), 255.

6 The Watchtower Bible and Tract Society, "The Peace and Unity of Jehovah's Witnesses," *The Watchtower* Jan (1960): 18-26.

7 "Do Jehovah's Witnesses Believe They Have the One True Religion?" https://www.jehovah's witness.org/en/jehovahs-witnesses/faq/true-religion/.

8 Ruth Tucker, *Another Gospel: Cults, Alternative Religions, and the New Age Movement* (Grand Rapids: Zondervan, 1989), 123.

[9] Ibid., 118.

[10] Gene Edson Ahlstrom, "The Church in the Thought of Charles Taze Russell," (M.A. thesis, University of California-Santa Barbara, 1990), 4.

[11] Ibid., 135.

[12] William Scriven, "Date-setting in America for the Second Coming of Christ During the Late Nineteenth and Early Twentieth Century," (Master of Arts diss., Andrews University, 1947), 42.

[13] Vivian Gornick, "A Witness Testifies," *The New York Times*, Nov 19, 1978.

[14] J.J. Ross, *Some Facts and More Facts About the Self-styled Pastor Charles T. Russell* (Philadelphia: The Philadelphia School of the Bible, 1912), 25-31.

[15] Sean McDowell, *Apologetics for a New Generation: A Biblical and Culturally Relevant Approach to Talking About God* (Eugene: Harvest House Publishers, 2004, Kindle Edition), 226.

[16] M. James Penton, *Apocalypse Delayed: The Story of the Jehovah's Witnesses,* 2nd edition (Toronto: University of Toronto Press, 2002), 47.

[17] Edmond Gruss, *The Four Presidents of the Watchtower Society: The Men and the Organization they Created* (Maitland: Xulon Press, 2003), 31.

[18] Penton, *Apocalypse Delayed*, 50.

[19] *The Watch Tower Society,* "How We Became Known as Jehovah's Witnesses," in *Jehovah's Witnesses—Proclaimers of God's Kingdom* (Brooklyn: The Watch Tower Society, 1984), 150-152.

[20] Gruss, *The Four Presidents*, 26.

[21] Ibid., 27-28.

[22] Penton, *Apocalypse Delayed*, 57.

[23] Rodney Stark and Laurence Iannaccone, "Why do the Jehovah's Witnesses Grow so Rapidly: A Theoretical Application," *Journal of Contemporary Religion* 12 (1997): 139.

[24] Bruce Metzger, "The Jehovah's Witness and Jesus Christ: A Biblical and Theological Appraisal," *Theology Today* January (1953): 67.

[25] Lucas Butler, "Trusting the Faithful and Discreet Slave: A Critique of the Authority of the Jehovah's Witnesses," (PhD diss., *The Southern Baptist Theological Seminary*, 2014), 11.

[26] Publishers are those members who are active in proselyting people by proliferating *Watch Tower* tracts and engaging others with the Jehovah's Witnesses' message. Based on this definition of a Publisher, by 1970, the Jehovah's Witnesses had around 1.3 million Publishers active in outreach. See M. James Penton, *Apocalypse Delayed: The Story of the Jehovah's Witnesses,* 2nd edition (Toronto: University of Toronto Press, 2002), 92.

[27] "How Many Jehovah's Witnesses Are There Worldwide?" https://www.jw.org/en/jehovahs-witnesses/faq/how-many-jw/.

[28] Ibid.

[29] Kevin Quick, *Reasoning with Jehovah's Witnesses: A Scriptural Study of the Teachings of the Jehovah's Witnesses* (Hydepark: Self-Published, 1986), 33.

[30] *Reasoning from the Scriptures,* The Watchtower Bible and Tract Society (Brooklyn: The Watchtower and Tract Society, 1985), 424.

[31] Butler, "Trusting the Faithful and Discreet Slave," 150.

[32] Metzger, "The Jehovah's Witnesses," 70.

[33] "What is the Holy Spirit?" https://jw.org/en/Bible-teachings/questions/what-is-the-holy-spirit/

[34] R.C. Sproul, *What is the Trinity?* (Grand Rapids: Reformation Trust Publishing, 2011), 59.

[35] Amber Scorah, *Leaving the Witnesses: Exiting a Religion and Finding Life* (New York: Penguin, 2020), 76.

[36] *The Watchtower Bible and Tract Society*, "What is Salvation?" https://www.jw.org/en/Bible-teachings/questions/what-is-salvation.

[37] "How does God Save Us from Death?" https://www.jw.org/en/Bible-teachings/online-lessons/basic-Bible-teachings/unit-3/god-save-us-death-ransom/#162

[38] "The Ransom—God's Greatest Gift," https://www.jw.org/en/lbrary/books/Bible-study/meaning-jesus-ransom-sacrifice/.

[39] "After Jesus's Resurrection, Was His Body Flesh or Spirit," https://www.jw.org/en/Bible-teachings/questions/jesus-body/

[40] Ibid.

[41] Don Malin, "The Watchtowers View of the Anointed and Great Crowd, https://watch-man-ga.org/the-watchtowers-view-of-the-anointed-and-great-crowd.

[42] *Reasoning from the Scriptures*, 361.

[43] Butler, "Trusting and Faithful," 99.

[44] Tucker, *Another Gospel*, 141.

[45] Tucker, *Another Gospel*, 124.

[46] Charles Taze Russell, *Studies in the Scriptures, volume 2* (Brooklyn: Watchtower Bible and Tract Society, 1888), 98-99.

[47] Ron Rhodes, *Reasoning from the Scriptures with Jehovah's Witnesses* (Eugene: Harvest House, 2009), 346.

[48] *The Watch Tower Bible and Tract Society*. "Millions Now Living Will Never Die" (Brooklyn: Watchtower Bible and Tract Society, 1920), 88-90.

Rhodes, Ron. Reasoning from the Scriptures with the Jehovah's Witnesses (p. 447). Harvest House Publishers. Kindle Edition.

[49] Butler, "Trusting the Faithful," 12.

[50] Rhodes, *Reasoning from the Scriptures*," 350.

[51] "The Cross," https://www.jehovah's witness.org/en/library/magazines/awake-no2-2017-april/the-cross-is-it-biblical/.

[52] Robin Jensen, "5 Myths about the Cross," *The Washington Post*, April 14, 2017. https://www.washingtonpost.com/opinions/five-myths-about-the-cross/2017/04/14/dae63c1a-1fa8-11e7-be2a-3a1fb24d4671_story.html.

[53] David Scaer, "All Theology is Christology: An Axiom in Search of Acceptance." *Concordia Theological Quarterly* 80 (2016): 49.

54 Ibid., 49.

55 Sinclair Ferguson, "Does Christology Matter?" https://www.ligonier.org/blog/does-christology-matter/

56 "2019 Grand Totals," https://www.jehovah's witness.org/en/library/books/2019-service-year-report/2019-grand-totals.

57 Quote is popularly attributed to Walter Martin, the author of *Kingdom of the Cults* (1965).

58 R.C. Sproul's response in a Q & A at the 2014 Ligonier National Conference. https://www.ligonier.org/learn/conferences/overcoming-the-world-2014-national-conference/questions-and-answers-2-2014-national/?.

CHAPTER 6: MAINLINE PROTESTANT LIBERALISM

1John Knox, "Friedrich Schleiermacher: A Theological Precursor of Postmodernity," *Church Life Journal.* November 23, 2018. https://churchlifejournal.nd.edu/articles/friedrich-schleiermacher-a-theological-precursor-of-postmodernity/

2 Robert Richards, "Cambridge Companion to the Origins of Species," edited by Robert Richards and Michael Ruse (New York: Cambridge, 2009), *xvii-xvii.*

3 Andrew Hoffecker, "The Rise of Protestant Liberalism," https://tabletalkmagazine.com/article/2019/05/rise-protestant-liberalism/.

4 E.F. Klug, "The Roots of Theological Liberalism," *Concordia Theological Quarterly* 44 (1980): 218-219.

5 Christopher Lensch, "Presbyterianism in America: The 19th Century: The Formative Years," *Western Reformed Seminary* (2006): 6-8.

6 Kenneth Parker, "The Rise of Historical Consciousness Among the Christian Churches: An Introduction," in *Studies in Religion and the Social Order,*" eds., Kenneth Parker and Erik Moser (Lanham: University Press, 2013), 10-11.

7 William Walker, "Demythologizing and Christology," *Forum* 3 (2014): 31.

8 Brent Hege, "Rudolf Bultmann on Myth, History, and Resurrection," Myth, History, and the Resurrection in German Protestant Theology / (2017): 47.

9 Christopher Kiesling, "Bultmann's Moral Theology: Analysis and Appraisal," *Theological Studies* 30 (1969): 225.

10 William Arnette, "Rudolf Bultmann's Existential Interpretation of the New Testament," *The Asbury Seminarian* 17 (1963): 34.

11 Joseph F. Flint, "Psychology for Preachers" (*The Biblical World* 13 (1899): 326.

12 "Overview," https://www.barnesandnoble.com/w/in-his-steps-charles-sheldon/1002266040

13 Amanda Conley, "Walter Rauschenbusch and the Social Gospel," *Denison Journal of Religion* 9 (2010): 6.

14 Walter Rauschenbusch, *The Social Principles of Jesus* (Amazon.com Services, Kindle Edition), 44.

15 Harry Emerson Fosdick, "Shall the Fundamentalists Win?" Transcripts of a sermon preached by Harry Emerson Fosdick May 21, 1922.

16 R.L. Torrey, *The Fundamental of Christianity* (New York: Dorian, 1918), 12.

17 *The Orthodox Presbyterian Church,* "What is the OPC?: Basic Information to Acquaint you with the Orthodox Presbyterian Church" (Willow Grove: The Committee on Christian Education of the Orthodox Presbyterian Church, 2013), 7-8.

18 Ibid., 7.

19 J. Gresham Machen, *Christianity and Liberalism* (Louisville: GLH, 1923), 44.

20 Owen Strachan, *Awakening of the Evangelical Mind: An Intellectual History of the Neo-Evangelical Movement* (Grand Rapids: Zondervan, 2015), 29-30.

21 Ibid., 41.

22 Ibid., 111.

23 "PCUSA Membership," https://layman.org/wp-content/uploads/2013/06/pcusa-membership-1960-20121.pdf

24 Bob Allen, "SBC Baptisms, Membership Number Falls," https://baptistnews.com/article/sbc-baptism-membership-numbers-fall/ However, the Southern Baptists have since then lost 1.3 million members, a loss of 8 percent. https://lifewayresearch.com/2020/06/04/southern-baptists-face-largest-membership-decline-in-100-years/

25 Benton Johnson, "Liberal Protestantism: End of the Road?" *The Annals of the American Academy of Political and Social Science* 480 (1985): 39.

26 Norman Geisler, "The Inerrancy of the Bible," https://www.namb.net/apologetics-blog/the-inerrancy-of-the-Bible/.

CHAPTER 7: THE PROSPERITY GOSPEL

1 Cost Hinn, "The Prosperity Gospel: A Global Pandemic," https://www.reformandamin.org/articles1/2019/1/8/the-prosperity-gospel-a-global-epidemic.

2 Ruth Tucker, *Another Gospel: Cults, Alternative Religions, and the New Age Movement* (Grand Rapids: Zondervan, 1989), 153.

3 G.A. Ludueña, "Mesmerism," Encyclopedia of Latin American Religions.

4 Mitch Horowitz, *Occult America: White House Seances, Ouija Circles, Masons, and the Secret Mystic History of Our Nation* (New York: Bantam, 2009), 82.

5 Stewart Holmes, "Phineas Parkhurst Quimby: Scientist of Transcendentalism," *The New England Quarterly* 17 (1944): 362.

6 William Atkinson, *The Spiritual Death of Jesus* (Boston: Brill, 2009), 79.

7 Essek William Kenyon, *Two Kinds of Faith: Faith's Secrets Revealed,* 10th edition (Seattle: Kenyon's Gospel Publishing Society, 1969), 60.

8 A.G. Butterworth, "E.W. Kenyon's Influence of the use of Scriptures in the Word of Faith Movement through the teachings of Kenneth E Hagin and Kenneth Copeland: A Dogmatic Study," (M.A. Diss, North-West University, 2012), 9.

[9] D.E. Harrell, *Oral Roberts: An American Life* (Bloomington: Indiana University Press, 1985), 461.

[10] Associated Press, "God Spared Him Because His Flock Raised $8 Million Dollars, Roberts says," *The Los Angeles Times*, April 2, 1987.

[11] Norman Vincent Peale, *The Positive Principle Today* (New York: Simon & Schuster, 1976), *ix*.

[12] Justin Wilford, "Televangelical Publics: Secularized Publicity and Privacy in the Trinity Broadcasting Network," *Cultural Geographies* 4 (2009): 512.

[13] John MacArthur, "Unholy Trinity." https://www.gty.org/library/articles/a392.

[14] Jim Bakker and Ken Abraham, *I Was Wrong* (Nashville: Thomas Nelson, 1996), 533.

[15] Matthew Schwartz, "Missouri Sues Televangelist Jim Bakker For Selling Fake Coronavirus Cure," https://www.npr.org/2020/03/11/814550474/missouri-sues-televangelist-jim-bakker-for-selling-fake-coronavirus-cure.

[16] Gloria Copeland, "I Need a New Car," https://www.kcm.org/au/node/14937.

[17] Joel Osteen, *I Declare: 31 Promises to Speak Over Your Life* (Philadelphia: Running Press.)

[18] R. Albert Mohler, "Would You Trade Eternal Life for a Ferrari? The False Gospel of Prosperity Theology," https://albertmohler.com/2019/05/03/would-you-trade-eternal-life-for-a-ferrari-the-false-gospel-of-prosperity-theology.

[19] John Stott, *The Message of the Sermon on the Mount* (Downers Grove: IVP, 1978), 132

[20] Millard Erickson, *The Concise Dictionary of Theological Terms* (Downers Grove: IVP, 2001), 65.

[21] John Piper, "Is there a Point to the Last Minutes of Suffering Before Death," https://www.desiringgod.org/articles/is-there-a-point-to-the-last-minutes-of-suffering-before-death?fbclid=IwAR2g0QtdyybAIggSb083ePMB-KVAERQr3RPi9UJe5hpEAg2k050ofjc6kRc8

AFTERWORD: RECOGNIZNG WOLVES

[1] "15 Key Quotes from J.C. Ryle's 'Warnings to the Church,'" https://www.mon-ergism.com/blog/15-key-quotes-jc-ryle's-"warnings-churches.

[2] Mike Nichols, director, 1988, *Biloxi Blues*. Universal Studios.

[3] Steven Cole, "Religion for Fun and Profit: 1 Timothy 6:3-5," a sermon. https://media-cloud.sermonaudio.com/text/9922516 2230341.pdf.

[4] Costi Hinn, *God, Greed, and the Prosperity Gospel: How Truth Overwhelms a Life Built on Lies* (Grand Rapids: Zondervan, 2019), 55.

[5] R.C. Sproul, *Matthew: An Expositional Commentary* (Orlando: Reformation Trust, 2013), 177.

APPENDIX A

[1] Joe Matthews, "The 'Bethel Effect': Redding mega-church a force for community building—and controversy," *Desert Sun*, March 14, 2019.

[2] The late theologian, Peter Wagner was more of the originator of the movement. However, the Johnsons are the modern popularizers of the movement with Bethel being the eye of the NAR storm.

[3] Nick Williamson, "A Critique of the New Apostolic Reformation (NAR) Movement's Claim that the Lost Office of 'Apostle' has been Fully Restored and Should be Acknowledged by Today's Church (Bachelors of theology diss, Queen's University-Belfast, 2016), 1.

[4] Ibid., 3.

[5] Ervin Budiselić, "The Problem of 'Kingdom Now' Theology Challenge, Part 1," *Biblical Institute Zagreb* October (2015): 146-147.

[6] "The New Apostolic Reformation and the Theology of Prosperity: The 'Kingdom of God' as a Hermeneutical Key," *The Lausanne Content Library https://www.lausanne.org/content/88558.*

[7] Julia C. Loren, *Supernatural Anointing: A Manual for Increasing Your Anointing*, Shifting Shadows Series (Shippensburg, PA: Destiny Image, 2012), 140-141.

[8] K. Thor Jensen, "Megachurch Trying to Raise Baby from the Dead through Prayer and Song While Raising Funds for Her Family," *Newsweek* December 12, 2020, https://www.newsweek.com/church-raising-100000-raise-child-dead-1478511.

[9] Ibid.

[10] Jessilyn Justice and Taylor Berglund, "Banning Liebscher: Why Bill Johnson Didn't Immediately Shut Down Grave Sucking," https://www.charismamag.com/spirit/church-ministry/36641-bethel-pastor-why-bill-johnson-didn-t-immediately-shut-down-grave-sucking.

[11] Randy Clark and Bill Johnson, *The Essential Guide To Healing: Equipping All Christians to Pray for the Sick* (Bloomington: Chosen, 2011), 125.

[12] Geerhardus Vos explains, "Christ's work as Mediator must possess an infinite value, since that work must extend to the satisfaction of the eternal wrath of God. A mere man can never endure this wrath, as is already apparent from the eternal punishment of those who are lost." Geerhardus Vos, *Reformed Dogmatics: Christology*, translated and edited by Richard Gaffin Jr. (Grand Rapids: Lexham, 2014), 33.

APPENDIX B

[1] *The Canon of Dort, 1618-1619,* "The Third and Fourth Main Point of Doctrine, Article 14: The Way God Gives Faith," https://www.crcna.org/welcome/beliefs/confessions/canons-dort?language_content_entity=en.

[2] *The Catechism of the Roman Catholic Church,* "Chapter One: The Sacraments of Christian Initiation," https://www.vatican.va/archive/ccc_css/archive/catechism/p2s2c1a1.htm.

[3] Ibid.

[4] George Mastrantonis, "The Fundamental Teachings of the Eastern Orthodox Church," https://www.goarch.org/-/the-fundamental-teachings-of-the-eastern-orthodox-church.

5 "How Does One Become A Member of the Church of Christ," https://www.church-of-christ.org/how-does-one-become-a-member-of-the-church-of-christ.html.

6 Tal Davis, "International Churches of Christ," https://www.namb.net /apologetics/resource/international-churches-of-christ/.

7 Bobby Ross, "'No Creed but Christ, no book but the Bible,'" https://christianchroni-cle.org/no-creed-but-christ-no-book-but-the-Bible/

8 Just consider one church affiliated with the ICOC, the Fort Wayne, Indiana Church of Christ; this church explains, "We believe that our salvation totally depends on the work of God and nothing of our own merit. That work of God is one of mercy and grace. That work redeems those who hear, believe, accept the Gospel message and repent (turn to God) and are baptized into Christ through their faith in God's power." https://www.fortwaynecoc.org/about.

9 "Articles of Faith," *The United Pentecostal Church International 2017 Manual.* https://upciminis-ters.com/attachment/document/mincom_212/2017midyearupcimanual.pdf?fileexten-sion=pdf.

10 Luther McIntire Jr., "Baptism and the Forgiveness in Acts 2:38," *Bibliotheca Sarca* 153 (1996): 57.

11 Mark Van Hart, "The Exodus as a Sacrament: The Cloud, The Sea, and Moses Revisited," *Mid-American Journal of Theology* 12 (2001): 43.

APPENDIX C

1 Philip Gardiner, *Secret Socities: Revelations about the Freemasons, Templars, Illuminati, Nazis, and Serpent Cults* (Franklin Lakes: New Page, 2007, Kindle), Location 609.

2 Christoph Riedweg and Steven Rendall, *Pythagoras: His Life, His Teaching, and Influence* (Ith-aca: Cornell Press, 2005), 98-99.

3 "Want to Join? Pythian Principles," *Grand Lodge of Knights of Pythias Indiana.* https://indi-anapythias.org/want-to-join/.

4 Gregory Wills, *The Southern Baptist Theological Seminary, 1859-2009* (New York: Oxford, 2009), 422.

5 "About Us," https://www.kappadeltaphinas.org/about-us

6 Hank Nuwer, "Hazing in Fraternities and Sororities," in *International Encyclopedia of the Social & Behavioral Sciences*, 2nd edition, edited by James Wright, (Amsterdam: Elsevier, 2015), 554-555; 559.

7 "About Freemasonry: Statement on Freemasonry and Religion," *Conroe Masonic Lodge.* https://conroe748.com/about-freemasonry/.